WHEN THE SUN

WAS A WINGED BIRD

(Journal of an Alcoholic's Wife)

Lily Knight

When The Sun Was A Winged Bird. (Journal of an Alcoholic's Wife)
Lily Knight

ISBN 1883707455

First Edition 2000 AD

Contact:
LightSlip.com
kaolink@msn.com
Phone: 770 242 9891

6920 Peachtree Industrial Blvd
Suite B
Norcross
Georgia 30071
USA

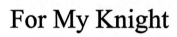

For My Knight

This story could happen every day somewhere and to anyone at any time - it happened to me.

The name of the beloved alcoholic husband, I shall call "Dion," after Dionysis, god of wine.

I, Dion's wife, have named myself "Rose," because Dion used to call me 'His Rose.' The first reason for this nickname was born in our early courtship when he observed that my lipstick was the color of a rose. Secondly, he often brought me a single red rose when I least expected it. But, the nickname became solidified one night as we watched his favorite video, The Little Prince. In the video, the Little Prince commented to himself regarding his beautiful, but self-centered Rose, "How can I tell her she's just another Rose? But, she is My Rose."

The third character in this story was Jessie. She was an intrusive enemy who manipulated him with such self-serving motives that she soon became his primary enabler! I have given her the name Jessie after the biblical wicked Queen Jezebel, whose final demise was to have her dead body laid out in public and eaten by dogs.

Because Jessie considered herself a model Christian, she remained in strict denial about her true motivations for making sure that my Dion had a steady supply of alcohol. Simply put, his continued drinking furthered her own selfish needs, which were to attempt to buy herself love and companionship.

There is one final character that is so minor to the story that I call him "the boyfriend." He was the boyfriend I was dating when I met my beloved Dion.

When I met Dion, he was 45 years of age and was nearly dead. He had managed to stay alive because he had a very strong will and because it was in God's plan for the two of us to meet. I met him shortly after he breezed into the church where Jessie conducted "missionary work" for street addicts.

But Dion, not your average street addict, was intelligent, had a sense of pride, and could support himself, when sober. He was a unique individual who quickly dazzled Jessie with his Scottish wit, his charm, and his ability to play beautiful music.

He played several instruments; but guitar was the one he kept by his side when everything else, piece by piece, had gotten hocked to buy alcohol. He was very protective of his guitar, however. And if ever he had to hock it temporarily, reclaiming it was the only thing that would motivate him to take a part time job driving a taxi, working in a grocery store, or pumping gas long enough to enable him to "get the 12-string out of hock."

I want this story to be told for Dion. He stumbled through his existence feeling as if he had never made a single contribution to life. But nothing could be further from the truth. Dion, despite his alcoholism, was the most deeply spiritual person I had ever met. Our

4

entire experience was deeply spiritual. Srom the moment we met, we both knew that this love had been ordained from the beginning of days.

I met Dion when I showed up to audition for his band. The story begins the night of the music audition that Dion held while still living at Jessie's house. I recognized as early as that first meeting that whereas Jessie hated me the instant she laid eyes on me, Dion and I loved one another at first sight. He was my True Heart, My Knight, my Other Half, my Twin Soul. Please read this story of the tragedy of alcoholism for what it truly is - a love story.

FEBRUARY ONE

February 16, 19__ - Saturday

Out of the blue appears to be good fortune; yet, too soon to tell. One minute I think success; one minute I think scam, one minute I think love. Dion introduced himself as a musician actually called me to audition for his band. But, his approach through the haze of alcohol seems sometimes unattainable. Weaknesses are - he has vision, but is short on execution. Part of the reason I say this is because he is nearly unable to communicate verbally (though he does it brilliantly on paper with words in songs he has written). In fact, with his badly slurred speech (I wonder how much alcohol he drinks to arrive here?) only do his written words show me he still functions coherently.

A little secret between you and me: he claims he wrote STANDING IN THE RAIN with me in mind. Claims he was set to leave town to go back to the beach, but he couldn't manage to leave me behind. He says as much as he hates cities; he stayed here so he could see me. Of course, I am flattered. The thing that scares me is that as a sideline, I have become enamoured of him too. I am in awe of this curiosity. He looked at me tonight and that thing was there. More puzzling, it was an old thing. It feels as if it has existed through the ages. This feels like it has existed for eternity.

Enough of drama. Were I functioning logically, I would agree that he is, to quote my boyfriend, "a drunk." His demeanor (being drunk, red-eyed, anti-social of sorts) verges on unacceptable. Simply said, he acts pretty eccentric. He resembles an extremely intelligent man who walks around in a hypnotic daze.

There is something in all of this that seems out of character for what he should be. Okay, why can't I accept (before I get myself in trouble) what my eyes see? What my head tells me? Why am I enamored? Simply this: I have come to love the spirit of the man. Yet, I don't trust myself and I wonder if I have merely invented the spirit? Is this a scenario I, myself create? Are these merely my own wanderings and fantasies? That could explain it. But, what troubles me is this: why this familiar feeling, this knowing? I know most people in my circle don't believe in reincarnation. I'm not sure I do either. I do believe we humans somehow agreed to this earthly assignment. All I can say is this: I have always been Dion's other half.

But, I must bury this new feeling of love in my heart and not act upon it. I have a boyfriend. Dion lives with Jessie and I don't know what their relationship is all about. He acts like she is his Mother, but she acts like he is her date: "Dion said this; Dion said that; Dion took me here; Dion took me there."

So, it's final: I will not tell him how I feel (except I did tell him with one look, as he told me). I will submerge my feelings in poetry. I told him, in fact, that I wrote poetry. He wants to read my poems. He mentioned he would like for us to produce a poetry-music tape, something along the lines of the old 60's poet, Rod McKuen, who recorded his poetry over the sounds of music and the sea. But, with Dion's slow, distracted, bourbon-misted behavior, the tape may never come to fruition.

One thing I feel certain: he is not a con. When he says he plans to do things, he does not intend to manipulate. I believe he truly plans these things. It is only his fragmented mind that prevents firm accomplishments.

So, what am I going on about? I can answer this: it is an oasis for my soul. That is how it feels.

February 22, 19__ - Friday

So much has happened in seven days. Tuesday, I had Dion over for dinner. We talked of our mutual attraction. It was such an easy thing to confess. Wednesday, we (the band plus Jessie, Mrs. Money Bags) left for the beach, arriving there very late after several aborted stops because (as I later found out) Dion wanted to ride with me and talk to me; but, Jessie would NOT allow it in any way. They were in her car (well, Dion doesn't have a car); and, it was obvious with each stop we made that there was huge quarreling behavior going on in their car. I was driving my car and bringing Steve, the singer. Neither one of us knew what the heck was going on with all those stop-and-shout matches.

Once we got to the beach Steve and I walked quietly up and down, listening to the waves while back in the condo, Jessie and Dion fought.

Dion had invited my boyfriend, but I couldn't dream of bringing him. My heart no longer belongs to my boyfriend; and, I knew I had to find a way to break the news.

Once inside the beach condo, I saw there were two bedrooms, so I assumed he and Jessie would sleep in one and the other had been earmarked for my boyfriend and me. This was not the case, however, as I found out when I lay down in the bedroom with the twin beds (stupid me thought Steve was going to take the other twin bed, I DON'T KNOW). Imagine my surprise when Jessie came in my bedroom all dressed up in her pajamas.

"Oh," I said when I saw her, "were you and Dion going to sleep in here? I just assumed you two would sleep in the double bed."

She gave a little laugh and said, "We don't sleep together."

With part of me, I breathe a huge sigh of relief; with the other, I chuckled as I thought, 'I forgot, you are running a Christian ministry.'

But, that night after I went to bed, Dion came into the room and called me downstairs for a private guitar concert. Jessie crept out of bed and positioned herself on the top of the stairs and sat watching us. You can imagine my shock when I looked up and spied her WATCHING me. It was very obvious that she had been trying to listen in on our conversation.

7

Our conversation had become pretty personal, as I found Dion telling me about how his Dad had met a woman he really loved when he was about Dion's age. He then told me, "I find myself in my Dad's place."

When Dion told me he loved me, I moved towards him on the couch out of Jessie's vision, and sat cradling his feet in my lap. We continued to talk. He told me he wanted to live on the beach with me. He said he had never felt so relaxed. As I caressed his legs and feet, he told me so many other things: he felt we were soul mates, I was beautiful, etc., etc., etc.

At 4:00 a.m., Jessie came downstairs looking very upset, so I quietly excused myself and went up to bed.

The next morning I looked in the mirror and despite having only four hours of sleep, I had never looked more beautiful. But, all hell broke loose the next morning when Steve and I went out to breakfast together to get away from the tension between Jessie and Dion. Stupidly, I confessed to Steve this troubling attraction between Dion and I.

Although Steve promised to keep it quiet, he went back to the condo and told Jessie that she and I had "things to discuss," so I told her all the things Dion had said to me. She marched straight upstairs into Dion's room, slammed the door and the next thing I knew, Dion had called a meeting with the four of us. He was furious about all this fuss. He said he loved only his music. Then he dismissed us all like we were so many little puppet servants.

This ridiculous fiasco convinced me to leave earlier than we had planned, so I asked Steve if he wanted to make the 6-hour drive back to the city with me. He agreed.

When Dion heard these plans, he pulled me outside; and, as we walked on the beach, he begged me not to leave. He said he knew a quiet little motel in town; he asked if I would go and meet him there. I said I didn't think it would be a good

I cried so hard during the 6-hour drive back to the city that Steve, feeling sorry for me, stopped at a service station where he bought a little plaque for me that said something like "wishing you love, faith and joy."

Once home, I couldn't get Dion out of my mind; couldn't forget his beautiful midnight concert played with that poignant sadness he wears everywhere. My feelings had nowhere to go, so I wrote him a poem:

Midnight Concert
Feeling the power of my enigma
Come to the end of the road,
All ways barred,
There you stand;
Gaze out to sea,
You strum your midnight concert to me.
Encasing the pain,
You hold stubborn the Scottish bent
To the chin.

Silent within
To all but notes clear
And sung
To me,
To the sea.

February 23, 19_ - Saturday

I understand from Jessie's other houseguest that Dion and Jessie are still at the beach. Seems that after I left, Dion got very angry with Jessie for "running everybody off." He went on a huge drinking binge that nearly killed him. He ended up vomiting blood all over the nice carpet in front of the sofa in the beach condo and had to be rushed to the hospital.

They expect Dion to be in the hospital a week or so. I have cried for two days; but have hidden my grief from my boyfriend. I have cried because I fear Dion may be dying. I have cried because I want to spend every waking moment between now and then with him. I have cried because Jessie is acting like MRS. HITLER and WILL NOT allow Dion and I to even talk to one another. Does she think she can force things to be the way she intends?

I have cried because I don't know what to do with all the beautiful things he said to me. I have cried because maybe Dion needs Jessie to take care of him. Someone needs to make him eat, take him to the doctor. The man I want to spend my life with is neither well nor sober; and, I am not free. This is a hopeless situation that I try hourly to give over to God.

February 24, 19__ - Sunday

Sunday morning I dropped off the musical equipment at Jessie's house. She and Dion still aren't home. But, the houseguest said they were expected in Sunday P.M. I told her to have Jessie call me the minute they arrive and let me know how Dion is.

What was I thinking? I should know Jessie wouldn't call me. After much hand wringing, I called over there at 11:30 p.m. Steve answered the phone. Said Dion was there. I asked to speak to Dion. His voice sounded faint. I asked how he was; he said he was travel-weary. I said I wished we could talk. He said he too wished we could talk.

I said, "Dion, I don't see how I can come back and be a part of the band."

He said, "Lets talk about it over dinner."

I said, "when, tonight?"

He said he would call me back at home. It is nearly 2:00 p.m. There has been no call. I will reach out no more. I definitely won't go around Jessie again. I don't like her. But, my heart feels peace about this Dion thing. At least he has good care with Jessie. Maybe I am the bad influence.

February 26, 19__ - Tuesday

It becomes clear that in life there must oftentimes be an acceptance of things as they are. There must be an awe of each day's renderings rather than a planned, predicted, presumed, preferred outcome. For only in the acknowledgement of what is does beauty live.

I have begged God to preserve Dion one more day. I have asked that all angelic intercessors gather around him and break this spirit of demon possession in the form of liquor and subconscious suicide. I have asked for help that his soul choose life rather than death. I have asked that God use me to help Dion become strong. I have asked for protection from temptations of control, perceived control, from manipulation both conscious and otherwise. I believe this life is a race begun in heaven and maintained in heaven without benefit of earthly eyes to see or ears to hear. Sometimes only the deep prompting of the heart can begin to break through earthly sludge.

February 27, 19_ - Wednesday

After talking with Dion Tuesday night and proposing to fast and pray until he quit drinking and choose life, he took me out for dinner last night. He was completely sober! I never mentioned it; but, he brought up the subject by saying, "haven't you noticed that my eyes aren't red?"

We went to a Japanese restaurant where he ordered in Japanese, no less (was that to impress me?). He can, when he wants to, take such command of his environment, yet he lives in another woman's house; and, it is questionable whose money he uses.

He asked me to marry him. This comes eight days after we admitted an attraction. He wants children. It is all too fast. The only reason I can find that he would make such an unrealistic proposal is that he believes he will die. Yet, he claims that he wants to get back in touch with Zen masters and other healers whom he claims healed him several years ago when he was given two weeks to live. Although he seemingly resorts to Zen to reestablish mental health, he claims to be a devout Catholic. One reason for asking me to marry him is that he doesn't believe in premarital sex. He believes in love; he believes in marriage; he knows God put us together. So do I.

I cannot communicate the uniqueness of all this. I am in the grip of something very strong and have been feeling it coming for almost six months now.

I have asked God to help me recognize my powerlessness over anything on earth regardless of what my earthly eyes tell me they see. But, there must be also a dawning in Dion's spirit; and, today my prayer is for this dawning. Never have I been more challenged to turn a matter completely over to God. I am not so confident about making such decisions on my own. These must be God's decisions.

February 28, 19__ - Thursday

After spending a virtually alcohol-free dinner and discussion with Dion Wednesday night, Thursday night was a kind of backslide. Dion had gotten word that his sister had attempted suicide. So, when I picked him up at 7:00 p.m., I was immediately put off (as always) by Jessie's complaining. She noticed he was yellow (complication of cirrhosis). Her frowning negativity set my serenity on edge so the evening was marked with tension.

We went to the music store; then we drove to find an Aikido Class that Dion wants to join in order to begin rehabilitative actions. But, after observing the instructor, Dion wasn't too impressed. His comment was, "the young instructor's clean white hands have never killed anyone; he is just dancing."

Following the class we sat in the car while Dion tearfully confessed how he had killed a man, a civilian, right after the Vietnam war, while he sat in a bar waiting for his Dad to pick him up. Apparently, in the bar he had endured taunts and verbal abuse from a belligerent, longhaired hippie who made fun of Dion's shorn military hairdo.

The man, continuing his verbal abuse, stood and encouraged a fight. Dion said he reacted instantly and violently and the next thing he knew, the heckler lay dead on the floor of the bar. The thing I find most ironic about this story is that at that time in Dion's life, he had not yet started drinking.

Dion told me this story in tears, feeling the guilt after all these years, especially in later learning the man had a wife and kids. He also cringed at his momentary coldness at seeing the man lying dead on the floor. He was so afraid, he said, that he had become like his Father.

After a night's sleep, I woke this morning determined to be there for Dion. He needs me. He isn't taking anything from me. He isn't altering my life in any way. I have searched my heart for the answer. Dion loves me. I love him back without expecting any kind of a future; but I want to be there for him in the shadow of his aloneness and impending death (if he doesn't stop drinking, and soon).

Most people are put off by Dion's intense personal manner. They don't bother to look closer, else they would see the twinkle when he smiles; they would hear the wisdom in his weighted words.

MARCH ONE

March 2, 19_ - Saturday

I waited all day today for Dion to call because I had told him I was free all day. But, he called late in the afternoon just about the time my boyfriend arrived at my house. However, my boyfriend's presence didn't prevent me from talking to Dion for an hour and half. Naturally, my boyfriend was furious. He pointed out that never in our five years together had we talked for an hour and half. He said my involvement with "that drunk" was excessive, compulsive, and inappropriate. Then he reiterated that everything I do is excessive (huh?). He said I am getting mixed up in something dangerous. On some level, I fear he is right. Dion may tell me beautiful and entertaining stories; but that may be all they are. They may be pure hallucinations for all I know.

One thing I do question - do I have time or health to waste on nonsense? Honestly, the main glaring fault about Dion that bothers me most is his total disregard for my time schedule. Everything revolves around his schedule.

March 3, 19_ - Sunday

Dion called today around 3:00 p.m. asking that I come over and see him, so I went over to Jessie's house. The band was there. Everyone treated me with such a cold shoulder that I immediately got the impression that I wasn't welcome. I quickly reasoned that it had been entirely Dion's idea that I come over. And, furthermore, he had obviously not bothered to inform anyone else about this invitation. After about 5 minutes in the deep freeze, I left.

No sooner did I get back home than Jessie called to apologize. Then she quickly opened up the subject of Dion. She said that he told her he had asked me to marry him. She tried extracting various committal comments from me; however, I told her nothing. Seeing that she wasn't getting very far in our "confidential-type" conversation, she advised me not to marry him. I sat there; wanted to laugh; thought, "when did you become so interested in MY welfare, Miss-Throw-Me-Off-Your-Property-Hypocrite?"

I am afraid to say too much to her. Something in my heart tells me not to trust her even though she wears a Christian cloak.

March 4, 19_ - Monday

This morning early, I went to see Dion. I knew Jessie would be at work. I waited outside for someone inside to turn on lights. Imagine my surprise when Dion came out dressed in jogging clothes with a bandana tied around his head. He was dressed for early morning exercise.

He was as surprised to see me, as I was to see him. He went back into the house, got two tennis racquets. We played tennis until it began to rain. We embraced in the rain.

We went back to the house, and hooked up the musical equipment.

12

He played and I sang. Surprisingly, I knew the words to every song he played. I left at 1:00 p.m. vowing to return at 6:30. He said, "I can't make it through one more night without you. I can't sleep."

At home, I received a call from my daughter who had been contacted by my boyfriend about my involvement with Dion. My daughter expressed extreme fear and concern for my actions. She told me that my boyfriend said I should be committed. He also said Dion was not a person but a demon, which demon was after my soul. She made me promise to break loose.

Tearfully, I called Dion back to tell him I couldn't come over tonight. I told him my family, those who know and love me, saw danger in this, saw me sickly attaching myself to a danger. His reaction surprised me. He was hurt, but he didn't fall apart. In fact, tonight was the first time I have known him to be rational and calm because of limited alcohol intake. My heart tells me that maybe his love is strong enough to overcome the addiction. So, have I made a mistake listening to others?

March 5, 19_ - Tuesday

The result of yesterday's phone call was devastating, as Dion ended up in the hospital. Seems he had attempted suicide with alcohol.

March 7, 19__ - Thursday

Still in the hospital, Dion is now off alcohol and is more reserved than I have ever seen him. I guess I have never really seen him completely sober. I visited him yesterday and he was angry. He said that now that he is sober, he could tell I don't really want to marry him. He said Jessie asked him to marry her. He says he is tempted to marry for security. But, he said he would rather marry for love; would "rather pump gas and be with the one he loved."

I called a Priest today to see about converting to Catholicism so we can marry in the church. The Priest said if Dion was regularly attending church (he isn't) we could get married anyway. He said that first we should get professional counseling to deal with the alcohol issues. He said marriage wouldn't solve them.

From the way Jessie controls Dion, I'm afraid she is going to move in on him and force me out. I know this sounds ridiculous since I am the one who aborted our beautiful beginning by telling him my family didn't approve of him. I also may have aborted Dion's self-imposed attempt at sobriety. He had evidenced a serious attempt at sobriety that morning he set out to start an exercise program.

I feel so helpless in all this. I feel paralyzed by not only my own fears, but also by all the turmoil surrounding the two of us. Why won't everyone LEAVE US ALONE! No one wants us to be together; yet, I have never shared such love. Jessie makes our meetings impossible. We are unable to talk without her breathing over our shoulder. We are unable to spend quality time together unless we meet in the park. Maybe we will just have to start meeting at my house and deal with my boyfriend for a change instead of Jessie.

March 12, 19_ - Wednesday

So much happens in such a short time. Is this common when the threat of death hovers near? Saturday was Dion's best day in the entire year I have known him. He was eating a lot; he was joking; we were laughing. He said he planned to check out of the hospital the next day. WELL! The next day, Sunday, I raced to the hospital right after church to find him near comatose. I asked the nurse what had happened. She said he had had a reaction to a strong nausea drug they gave him. He said he got sick after eating a turkey sandwich. But, whether it was food or drug, the episode threw him into a combination liver/pancreas attack that nearly killed him. The points on his chart looked like Mount Everest in their plunge from recovery to near death. He also suspected he reacted to the Darvon they gave him.

I spent the night at the hospital as he literally hung on to life by a tiny thread, perspiring and writhing in pain despite shots of Demerol. By the morning he was resting easy; and, I left, vowing to return ASAP.

I returned to the hospital around 11:30 a.m. to see Jessie waiting in the room. I went in anyway, though she said not one word to me (and vice versa). I stayed there until 2:00 p.m. when she finally got up, kissed him goodbye, and left. He was still in pain, but felt slightly better. They had taken him completely off Demerol (for obvious addictive reasons) so although he was in pain; I suspect it had subsided since he was able to tolerate it with Darvocet alone.

I crawled into the hospital bed and we cuddled, even though he was all hooked up to wires. Fortunately, I didn't stay there long because shortly after I regained myself and moved to the chair, the Priest came by to speak with Dion about AA. Then I left at 4:00 p.m.

Dion had asked me to spend the night again. He said he didn't want Jessie there; said he would rather be alone. But, my boyfriend is becoming increasingly testy about "the amount of time you are spending with that drunk." I so want to say, "They are the happiest hours of my day," but I cannot find the words.

After searching my heart, I decided I must be completely honest to everyone involved if I am to do the right thing. So, Tuesday, as Dion lay in the hospital bed, I went looking for a small, affordable place to move Dion into. I tried explaining to my boyfriend that our relationship has ended. I said things really haven't been right for a long time. He knows it too. He just won't admit it. It's funny how when we begin to return disinterest with disinterest, we find ourselves on the road to the end.

When I returned to tell Dion about the apartment-hunting excursion, he refused to consider moving into a place that I pay for. I told him it wasn't my intent to pay for it. He has a source of income: concerts. But, as long as he is being supported without having to work for anything, he will continue to become weaker and weaker until he will no longer be able to find within himself the strength to do anything.

"Get away from Jessie while you still can," I said. "She is imprisoning you. Haven't you noticed how quick she is to throw everyone else out of her house that won't work and pay rent. Yet, she lets you stay there for free." And, in addition, she buys you everything you want (including alcohol, except I didn't say that last part).

He didn't comment. He just frowned. All I can do at this point is pray God will heal him; then wait for the answer. In the meantime, I need to attend Al Anon and seek to convert to Catholicism.

March 13, 19_ - Thursday

The search continues; God continues to speak; miracles happen. After spending a terrifyingly boring day at work, I went to the house to wait for Dion, as we had planned, to attend his AA and my Al Anon meeting together. All day I had prayed he had not had a relapse. I waited in the park behind Jessie's house until 7:20 p.m. (our plan); then left for the meeting. But, he surprised me by paging me and we ended up at the same meeting although not in the same car. He drove Jessie's car. I'll bet she doesn't know he is meeting me.

Sober, Dion has a reserve and coldness to the eyes that puts me off a bit. My old, insecure self begins to question - does he love me or is the booze just making him emotional? He answered my questions (though unasked by me) by saying he felt the way to show his love was to "provide for me; therefore, he is focused right now on making money in his music."

Now, I could at this point launch into all kinds of side roads: is music your main priority as you stated when we were all at the beach? Are you still planning to marry me? Blah, blah, blah. But, these thoughts are just of a lower grumbling. Truth is: I love Dion no matter how he feels toward me and no matter what he does or does not do to or for me. And, I must not lose sight of the reality that: sober, I have a life with him. Drinking, he may die. I can never hold him again if he is dead.

After the meeting, we talked briefly in the parking lot. He seemed anxious to see how the meeting affected me, asking me if this was my first meeting. I said no. I asked, "do you want to go somewhere get some coffee, something?" He surprised me by saying, "I don't want to make a late night of it. I have an early morning of work scheduled. I am serious about finding a way to provide for you."

March 15, 19_ - Saturday

Things have gotten crazy fast. I don't know how much of this is Dion's manipulation or my own interpretation. Friday, Dion called me earlier to see if I could meet him later. But "later" (he called at 8:30 p.m.) was too late for me, so we ended up talking on the phone at length.

Saturday, we met at the Indian Restaurant, and then drove to a music bookstore. Minus the alcohol, he is extremely quiet, physically distant; says after all these years of being alone, he actually forgets he can touch someone.

Sunday, he called me early. We met in the park; but, since it was

15

cool, we sat in my van and talked. He said he is trying to work very hard at healing his sick body; had to control his pulse rate with biofeedback. He had managed to get away from Jessie for an hour. He circled two apartments in the paper for me to check on for him to rent; asked me to call about them and call him back. Then he left; said he was going to check on the guitar; that he would be back.

I was furious. These side trips where he calls me over, talks to me for 5 minutes then leaves, make me crazy. I waited 30 minutes, all the time the clock in my head said I should be expected to wait. I came home. He called an hour later; asked how I was. I said I was furious that he had left me stranded; angry that he was very generous about my time. I suspected he was telling neither Jessie nor me the truth. He said that was all my interpretation; that he went to the house to make a phone call to check about the guitar repair; that Jessie came in; he had a bleeding attack; he gathered some things for me and came back to find me gone.

Then he told me the only reason he seemed to be holding back was because his health had worsened; said he didn't want me to come to depend on him and then he die.

March 17, 19_ - Sunday

This morning at church I had a prompting in my heart to call Dion. When he answered the phone, I told him I would be over to pick him up at 10:30 a.m. I knew the coast would be clear because Jessie would be in church until around noon.

We went to lunch at a Thai Restaurant; then I took him to a classical guitar concert. We began the day very quiet; but, over lunch, we talked about so many things. The day ended as beautifully as it had begun. We even looked at apartments together. We walked around downtown for blocks and blocks, held hands and fell more in love than ever. He looked so handsome in his brown tweed jacket, his long blonde hair just grazing his shoulders, the twinkle in his eye when he smiles. When we hold hands we look like the same person because our skin (Celtic, both) is exactly the same color. It is only my hair and eyes, which are dark. He said he was writing a song in his heart called, SOMETIMES LOVE IS ONLY A BLOCK AWAY.

March 21, 19__ - Thursday

After 4 days of sobriety, Dion started drinking again; and, although I am so disappointed, there is nothing more to be said on the subject. I told him last night that I would have no more to do with him while he was drinking. Then, I go running over there and spend all morning with him today.

I got a blood test today. I plan to marry him (like a fool). With him drinking again, he may not live long enough to do so.

He fixed breakfast for us this morning while Jessie worked. I feel so ill at ease in her dark, depressing house that my stomach turns and I can hardly eat food.

After breakfast, we went to the VA dentist where he told me war

16

stories of Viet Nam while we sat in the dentist's waiting room talking and laughing.

March 23, 19_ - Saturday

The crap really hit the fan yesterday. After a long day at work, I got a call from Dion saying he had bought a house; would I come by and look at it. So, at 11:30 p.m. (I am loosing sleep and weight like crazy!) I went over to Jessie's to pick him up to go look at the house.

It is a nice little house. He seems to have no fear about affording it. Anyway, seems that Jessie, shocked by his latest attempt at self-sufficiency, pulled out all the stops. As Dion and I sat in the car outside his 'new house', working on the song he wrote Sunday, I received a page (it was now 1:00 a.m.) from my daughter who was extremely upset because she had gotten an "anonymous" phone call from some "crazed woman" who indicated I might be in some kind of trouble. Shaking in my boots from anger, I told Dion what had happened. He turned extremely pale and said, "I'm sorry, Rose. The last thing you need is more stress because of me. Forgive me."

Jessie had gotten what she wanted. I had no recourse except to drive him back to her house.

Once home, I called my daughter and tried to talk to her; but, she screamed and said something like, "you're every bit as sick as that hopeless alcoholic."

APRIL ONE

April 7, 19__ - Monday

The biggest fiasco of a lifetime has occurred. My heart is broken and I even believe I am losing my mind. On March 24, Dion decided to move out of Jessie's house. His house deal wasn't going to happen for obvious reasons (I figured it was more or less a pipe dream). However, he had booked a room in a motel where we spent three glorious days together.

Although up to this point we had kissed and held one another, this was the first time we had made love. To think, I was actually intending to remain celibate until we were married! But, that shows me how much I love this man.

Dion obviously recognized that we were living lives of deceit by meeting in the park and talking on the phone during other people's absences. He wants as much as I do to come out into the open with our love affair. WE LOVE EACH OTHER. What is wrong with that except that it inconveniences other's plans? We aren't doing anything wrong. Besides, neither of us is married. He isn't married to Jessie; and, I am not married to my boyfriend. We are doing nothing wrong by being in love; so, why continue to sneak around as if we were?

Well, as to the three glorious days in the motel: despite the reality of his coming down off alcohol and being very ill, he was still the most wonderful lover. Maybe I say that just because he is so dear to me; he is truly my other half. No, it was more than that. We belong together.

Tuesday, our second day, he began to eat well; and, Wednesday we even went for a stroll in the mall near the motel. I was so proud to be with him. He looked very handsome. We had grown extremely close after three days together. But, our money ran out. I had to go back to work; and, he went reluctantly back to Jessie's. Naturally, Thursday he was drinking again.

He called Sunday to say let's get a room for Wednesday night. At the last moment, we got a room for a week. The first night, Wednesday, was glorious. We spent 3 or 4 hours making love. Thursday, he went back to Jessie's for money; the drinking began again after much arguing and strife that hangs around her. They must have fought until 9:00 p.m. because that is when he came back to the room. We had dinner at Red Lobster and went back to the room; but, by now I was upset at this intrusion, at being left alone in a strange room while he tried to extract money from Jessie.

Friday was more of the same; and, I told him Saturday as he kept pressing me to marry him that if he continued to drink, I couldn't feel good about marrying him. We are on such a merry-go-round.

Sunday, he talked to me. Said everything is changed without me; that he has no reason to go on. (I feel the same way). He said Jessie arranged for him to play at a concert, but he refused to do so because he said her plans come with a condition: Rose is not invited. I could tell he was extremely stressed from fighting with Jessie over her non-acceptance of me in his life. His behavior is so up and down and crazy. My behavior is also becoming crazy, as my emotions are up and down too. I can't even keep up with them.

Today, at Dion's request, I ventured over to Jessie's to pick him up. She stared daggers at me and I could tell that he had not told her that I would be by to pick him up. I could tell she had no idea how close we have become. So, I put Dion on the spot right in front of her. I pressed him; point blank asked him if we were still getting married. He said he cancelled plans to get a house (wrong, he has no money to buy the house). He said he wanted me to continue therapy (he needs therapy too). He said he wants me to join the Catholic Church; and on and on. It became obvious to me that he wasn't prepared to explain to Jessie our commitment. Why should he? He told her once that he was leaving ("declared us" as he puts it); that we planned to marry; and, I pulled the rug out from under him by listening to everyone around me but myself. Although I ended up crawling back to him, it wasn't until after I told him, "Everyone who knows and loves me feels this is a mistake." Jessie has merely been cashing in on my insecure vacillation.

But, I was so angry at his hedging that I called him "the biggest f_____ con I have ever met," (shocking words for their Christian ears, I am sure). I walked out, slammed the door and he has not called. Obviously, he is as glad to get away from my moods as I am to get away from his drinking. If only we could function as normal people. We would have the greatest love ever. The emotion is certainly there, but the maturity isn't.

April 27, 19_ - Sunday

I forgot what happened in between; but, on April 15, after my 11:00 therapist appointment, I departed with Dion and Steve, the singer, for the 5-hour trip to the beach, where Dion told Jessie we were going to rehearse. Seems the only way Dion can get away from her is to travel to the beach. He is assured she won't follow him to the beach because she hates the beach.

We pitched a tent on an island and for 6 days we loved and fought - we sleeping in the tent; Steve sleeping in the van; all of us rehearsing music in the daytime.

April 20, I had to come back to keep my therapist appointment. Dion and Steve stayed there and I PROMISED Dion I would be back. He reluctantly believed me; but, good for my word, I traveled back to the beach the next day. By this time, Dion had rented us a room - no more staying in the tent. It was good to get a bath. The campgrounds had showers but the weather had been cold and rainy; and, I froze the whole time I showered in the clubhouse, so the room was a welcome change.

But, we were forced to come back home the next day because between food, gas, and room expenses, we had run out of money.

Admittedly, after spending a week together, we began to trust and

19

communicate more; although we had a huge fight coming home. He had taken me to a church built in the 1700's, gotten down on his knees and asked me again to marry him. I answered him the way my therapist had advised: "I will make a commitment to marry you if you will make a commitment to get into treatment and quit drinking."

He finds ways around getting into treatment whether it is to say he will and then never follow through; or whether it is to deny he is drinking by hiding his alcohol, etc., etc.

He was so angry at my reply that he said, "That is the last time that I will ever ask you to marry me." But, the insanity wears thin; and, I wonder if I will lose respect for him and stop loving him.

Today is a perfect example of an intolerable fiasco. We had planned (because I like to plan and he likes to do things at the last minute) that I would come by and pick him up and go to church. Later we would go shopping; then to the theatre.

He called at 11:00 a.m. I said, "I was just on my way to pick you up."

He said he had been up all night because someone had stolen Jessie's credit cards. (Do I believe this? I don't think so. But, who is the liar? Jessie? Because she knows we had plans? Or Dion because he has other plans?) He said to call back at 2:00 p.m.

I called at 2:00 p.m. to say, "I'm on my way to pick you up." He said, "make it 3:00 p.m." It was pouring rain and I was raging inside and wanted to say something nasty like, "Forget it. I'm not going to spend time with you when you are this drunk." But, fortunately I didn't. However, when I called at 3:00 p.m. there was no answer. I decided to leave a calm, rational message: let him see the results of his drunken decisions; or, (translated without sarcasm: let him assume the consequences and responsibility for his own actions). So I said, "this is Rose. Sorry I missed you. I'm going to church tonight."

On my way to church I received a page from him. I called him back on my failing cellular and said, "Sorry, didn't get your message. I must get going. Sorry time got away."

He said, "I wish you wouldn't talk to me this way." Then the cellular died.

So, I am left not knowing if I did a good thing by attempting to hold up a mirror and show him the consequences of his choices;

OR

did I do a self-righteous, judgmental, martyrdom, holier-than-thou thing by expecting him all day to dance to my music?

At any rate, the union drives me nuts. I suspect it does the same to him. Something is eating at him. Is it all worth it? Am I creating my own problems? Can I change? Will he change?

MAY ONE

May 11, 19_ - Sunday

Dion brought me roses and a beautiful Mother's Day Card that said:
I love you so much that it's hard to remember
what my life was like before you were in it.
We've shared some pretty great times,

And even when times weren't so great,
I always knew I could count on you
For support and understanding.
You've been a comforting constant
In a totally unpredictable world....

And though I think you already know
How important you are in my life,
I could never say it too many times --
Thanks for being you.
You mean the world to me.

He signed it, "To a Beautiful Mother, All my love, Dion."

Near the 1st of May, I found an apartment for Dion. You can't imagine what a battle it was for him to manage to get his clothes (not to mention any of the musical equipment) out of Jessie's house. I pulled up in the van that day to load everything and they were in the middle of a screaming battle. All I could hear of the conversation was Dion yelling at her, "Why? Because I'm in love with another woman?" She wouldn't even come outside because Steve was helping load the van. He despises her as much as I do. He says she, in her selfish involvement with Dion, has even tried to run HIM off.

This day Miss Jessie was clearly outnumbered. All of her previous threats to Steve and I lay pretty much impotent this day with Dion trying to extract himself from her. Of course, as well as I know the softhearted Dion, I feel sure there will be some sort of reconciliation with her later.

She kept trying to jerk things out of Dion's hands saying they were hers because she paid for them. I began to feel badly and said to Dion, "She's right. She really did buy them for you." In answer to that, he said something under his breath to the effect that she was just using him so why couldn't he use the equipment.

Sick, sick stuff. Troubling stuff. Why can't we all act as adults? Why can't Jessie accept that Dion and I love one another? Why can't she be our friend? Once, she was so hip on trying to promote Dion to make money, but it is clear that her rules change when other people become involved with Dion. What does she want? A little musical puppet? Can't she see he is miserable around her?

If the 1st of May was a nightmare, the next several days that followed were pure hell. She called ALL the time. We tried unplugging the phone and when we checked messages, there would be about 5 or 10 calls from her. Some would say things like, "Dion, this is Jessie, give me a call." Oftentimes the messages would be just hang-ups. Sometimes after hours of having the phone unplugged while we would be practicing, she would just show up and bang on his door. After only two days of this kind of harassment, Dion began to drink again. Needless to say, I am dying inside. The only happy times are when he is on his deathbed (as he gets when he even takes one drink these days). He spends three days recovering. Then he goes back around Jessie, gets money and drinks. Lately, he has been having her either buy groceries or take him out to eat because without him working; and with me ignoring my work so much these days, money has become very tight. I must stop spending and go back to work. He has tried getting several music jobs; but, he can't stay sober long enough to convince anyone to hire him.

Sometimes I believe Dion couldn't love me or he wouldn't put me through this. Other times, I consider what kind of hell he must be going through. There is no telling what he has to tell Jessie to get her to continue to buy him all kinds of books, food, supplies, and tools. It is insane. Sometimes he begs me to leave this city and move with him to the beach. My answer is always the same: let's get out of debt first.

May 25, 19_ - Sunday

Our battles worsen. Whereas I once stayed in the apartment and slept with Dion overnight, lately I run from him to my own home where I lock the door, unplug the phones, barricade myself alone with my four animals and turn on the bathroom fan to drown out any door banging. He isn't violent. He is simply determined that I remain by his side. Yet, he won't tell Jessie to quit calling. She barges in. He even hid my nightgown once when she had been over there. Could it be that he needs for her to pay June's rent?

I know this latest battle is over money. The day began with him becoming angry that I wouldn't give him money for a drink. Jessie, his prime enabler lies in the hospital and he is all out of money. So, this morning when he informed me that he was getting angry because I was so "selfish," I ran from the car as soon as his back was turned; and, by some miracle, I managed to walk the 15 miles home. He has called once to try to lure me into conversation. But I stand firm: until he quits drinking, we cannot have a relationship.

May 30, 19_ - Friday

Today I finally returned Dion's phone call. I called to say I would stay with him only if he began an in-house alcohol treatment program. He refused. Yesterday, it seems he had begun a tapering off program for himself that ended as every other new attempt ends: him falling down drunk by 6:00 a.m. (his new bedtime). Since he has no car; was completely dependent on Jessie's car; and since I am now refusing to see him since he won't commit to SOME kind of treatment, I did give him a ride back over to Jessie's where he probably should have never left in the first place. She is willing to foot his astounding expenses; I am not.

Since I feel responsible for loving him and moving him away from

22

her thinking I could help him (I believed him when he said he couldn't make it one more night without me), I haven't the heart to leave him stranded without an explanation. So, I essentially made him choose. Is it alcohol? Or, is it I?

He was more docile than I had anticipated. He expressed continued love for me and continued hope. But, I have lost all hope. The situation is utterly impossible with its continual waste of time in search of the drink; with its endless procrastination spent accomplishing nothing; and the merry-go-round of near death experiences. The staying up all night is the worst nightmare of all. The man is truly caught in hell. He is ruled by mighty powerful demons that live inside the bottle.

Later, he showed up at my house in Jessie's car (wonder where he told her he was going) crying and begging me to come back to him.

JUNE ONE

June 2, 19_ - Monday

Friday when I dumped Dion at Jessie's house, I made concrete plans to turn around my life. I vowed to work more and I checked into going into a better-paying field (nursing). My Therapist discouraged me from nursing, however. I guess she could see the nursing binge was nothing more than the temporary, quick fix solution I am so famous for. She said the field of nursing requires tremendous commitment.

Saturday, I went back home and installed phone block on my telephone in an effort to block out all calls from Dion AND Elsie. But, Sunday found me unable to stay away from Dion. I missed him so. I went back to his apartment, for which I have a key. Was I surprised to find a dramatically changed Dion. He said he had turned back to God. Through a tearful confession he agonized how he wanted me in his life. He questioned how he could have allowed himself to open his heart to love me; lamented that the decision brought him only pain. He said those were eyes better not opened; said that before he had me in his life he had found a way to "manage;" but, said that now that he has known me he finds his life completely meaningless without me. He said at this low point he realizes he still has God. He said he was trusting that with God's help, all things are possible.

When Dion talks this way, it is obvious to me that he is not the problem; he is merely caught up in the problem. We are both to blame for the same problem. He finds me as impossible to live with as I do him. But, I am convinced it is not Dion who is impossible to live with; and, it is not Rose who is impossible to live with. They are two beautiful creatures that God created to love one another. It is the third party, the Demon, who makes it impossible for these two people who love each other, to function. The Demon is a separate entity that lives in the bottle. He is given birth when He is let out of the bottle. That bottle is best left uncapped because the Demon gives rise to lies, deception, and even creates a third demonic entity.

Tears fell from Dion's eyes as he talked and I knew that he had faced something frightening. For this one moment, I could see light. I could see hope. But, I also knew that in order to attain success, this one moment would have to be repeated tomorrow and the next day. I knew that for today the two of us had won a battle. The scary part was that I didn't know (nor did he) about tomorrow.

I ended up staying with Dion Saturday night fully expecting him to return to alcohol. Sunday, however, he didn't drink. He avoided Jessie like the plague all day Sunday. I stayed again Sunday night.

This morning I left Dion's apartment fairly early in order to accomplish several "must-dos." I must generate some money. I may even have to sell the van to raise $4,000 to pay bills.

After doing all my chores today, I went back to Dion's apartment,

24

but he wasn't there. While I was at his apartment, I answered the ringing phone to hear him say he was on the way back home. He asked me to please stay there until he got there. I stayed until 9:30 p.m. Finally, I gave up and went to a movie. Naturally, I assumed he would be drinking. However, he called me at my house around 11:00 p.m., very nice, very sober, expressing disappointment that I had gotten up early this morning; left him sleeping; and, didn't tell him where I was going. He doesn't trust me.

June 3, 19_ - Tuesday

This morning I went by his apartment on my way to my therapist. We had a brief (well, not all that brief) lovemaking session. Today is another day apart from him and I am on pins and needles hoping he won't drink.

Our love is so deep. I asked the therapist why it depresses me so much to be around him. She said it was because I became responsible for too much.

June 24, 19_ - Tuesday

I've had enough of Dion's abuse. Sober, he is cold; drunk, he acts crazy. I don't exactly mean cold (that is Jessie's word for him); he just seems so afraid of his feelings when he is sober. He will sit for hours and not say much. He blames this "frozen heart" on never having properly grieved his Father's death. No matter how much I love him, I find this vacuum frightening. I know he loves me. I can sit in the same room and feel it. So, why do his silences scare me? Is he too closely mirroring my own self-doubt? Am I not convinced that I am loveable? Do I not feel worthy of being loved?

Loveable or not, however, I need him to be sober. We can learn to communicate in this new silence. I can learn to love myself. He can learn to verbalize. However, continued drinking will put him only in the grave.

Jessie acts like she doesn't understand all this. She asked me once, "Have you ever seen Dion sober?"

At the time, the question puzzled me.

"No," I answered.

She frowned and said, "he's cold. And his music is not good."

I felt like screaming at her: "Do I hear you correctly? Are you saying you prefer him "musical" to the exclusion of sober? Doesn't this smack of some form of usury to your ears? It certainly does to mine."

Jessie must wake up and realize how hard she works to keep Dion in a place where she has control of the puppet strings. Dion must wake up and realize he has to stop depending on Jessie in any way. By depending, he relinquishes complete control to her; and, she does not have his best interest at heart. I must wake up and realize I can wake up neither Jessie nor Dion. The denial MUST stop or we all lose.

Dion is truly trying to turn his life around. But, his turnarounds seem to last about one month. Even as we draw closer together daily, this threat that hangs over our heads makes me very unhappy. Sometimes it seems completely hopeless. I tell him often that I can't take it anymore. He accepts this as a rejection of himself, the man.

As I expected, one night away from him and I miss Dion terribly. Much of my lonely longing is probably that old emotional void created as an abandoned infant. But, I don't want to get into that. Nevertheless, according to my therapist (and the vote is still out as to whether I like this therapist or not) without Dion to mirror my own despair (he, the alcoholic becomes the despair) and I don't have to feel the despair. I simply assign it to him. But, without Dion in the picture to play out the despair role, I feel it and the void becomes unbearable.

This psychobabble may all be true. But, I recognize another truth: I genuinely love Dion. Were I to reason for myself I would deduce, all dark Freudianism aside, when Dion is gone from my life I MISS him; I LONG for him; I GRIEVE his absence. To quote Dion himself, "you are my true heart."

With all of this agony boiling up inside me, I did something horrible this morning. I went to Dion's apartment early and found him sleeping (passed out is more like it). I smelled his breath and the alcohol was so strong that I knew he and Jessie had been out all night in his favorite bar: she paying, he drinking.

I decided to trash the apartment in search of alcohol and money and confiscate both. I found $17 in his coat pocket, which I stuffed in my purse. I also found his half-full Schnapps bottle, which I threw outside in the Dumpster. Even as I tossed the bottle in, in back of my mind I knew it would do no good. He would manage to get another $17 and another bottle as soon as he woke.

Looking back to his latest binge, I could have been prepared for it had I not ignored the signals. Last Sunday he said he was in pain; he was short and irritable with me saying things like, "You didn't appreciate my music so I took it away," meaning he quit playing the guitar or even the radio.

Of course, we have had a long-ongoing argument over music because he plays it several decimeters too loud and this alone has sparked two "noise complaint" warnings being taped by the apartment management to his apartment door. He also said that I made him feel "ugly."

He has a drinking pattern that goes like this: he drinks to excess; nearly dies; stops drinking in the "dying" stage; begins to feel better (the one good day we have each month); begins to get irritable and find fault; begins to drink again. Never have I entertained less hope than I do now. Despite all the fancy lies, all the reasons to quit, all the good intentions for church and AA, he cannot seem to break the cycle.

JULY ONE

July 1, 19_ - Tuesday

Thursday, I worked until 6:00 p.m.; then drove to Dion's apartment. He wasn't home; but Jessie dropped him off around 7:00 p.m. Although he and I passed the evening in a fairly civil manner, he had that "Jessie" attitude all over him as strong as the smell of her house - mothballs, strong strawberry potpourri, mold, and dust.

He, having been drinking fairly heavy, as he always does when in her company, fell asleep around 2:00 am. I left and slept at home.

Dion is angry with me because I left him alone; and, I am angry with him because he won't stay away from Jessie and quit drinking. He thinks I don't want to marry him; and I think he isn't serious about marriage or he would change. One of us MUST become the adult. Sometimes I think my compulsive need to be immature is as deeply rooted as his compulsive need to drink.

Friday, I prepared for my huge garage sale. When Dion picked me up at my place near dusk, I was disgusted by his drunken stupor. The night escalated into a serious battle with both of us calling each other the dirtiest names we could dream up. Again, he fell asleep around 2:00 a.m.; and, I left for home.

Dion misreads my disgust for his habit as a total disgust for him. He says I make him feel ugly. We cannot seem to rise above these destructive roles.

Saturday, fully intending to pull out all of my stuff from his apartment, I suddenly had a change of heart and when he called, I told him that all I knew to do was to start over.

Sunday was the day I had hoped he would go light on booze. We had planned to attend church at 6:00 p.m. He was supposed to pick me up at 5:30. I even got ready. He called to say "rehearsal" was running over. Just hearing the phony rehearsal-word set me off to an instant boiling point.

This so-called "music" scene has become somewhat of a joke. Shortly after I left the "band" I observed that when he engaged in his "music," he became morbid, sad, and in obvious emotional pain. I asked him to please put the music down and begin treatment. I even wrote a poem (actually a song) for him entitled:

PUT THE GUITAR DOWN

With your lips you say you love me;
With your hands you take your life.
You're a walking man, dying;
Yet, you want me for your wife.
Our time is short together

If we travel on this way.
There's so much I need from you
To share with me today.

CHORUS:
Put the guitar down, down;
Let's walk in the sand;
Put the guitar down, down.
Come hold my hand.
Tell the darkness around you;
It'll have to wait.
Put the guitar down, down
Before it's too late.

You've seen the mute dark angel
That lives inside the song.
You've watched the spirits bring you,
Your dooming soul along.
Now, reach beyond and take my hand
Across the great abyss
And give your vow to ride upon
The cherished wedding kiss.

I had hoped that my song would speak to Dion's heart, as my droning words had not been able to as yet. But, he got angry with me and said something like this: "At least Jessie encourages me to do the music. You want me to stop the music! Don't you know the music is who I am? If you don't like the music, you don't like me."

He also said things such as, "everyone sees me but you." "You don't realize how talented I am, I share my true self with you and you are miserable," etc., etc., etc.

Where his music is concerned, it doesn't take a digit above an idiot to see that we are not communicating. I DON'T want him to stop the music. I just want him to stop hiding behind the music. At any rate, Jessie uses this for all it is worth. She has set herself up against me as the "music advocate" versus me, the "music hater." She continually reminds him that, "Rose doesn't even like your music." Thus, the gap widens.

So imagine my despair to hear him say that, "rehearsal is running over." I clearly know there is no band; there are no music plans going on. Music is merely the Jessie buzzword. Rehearsal means: Jessie-is-paying-for-dinner-so-I-can-have-a-drink-on-Sunday-the-blue-law-can't-buy--liquor-any-other-way-day.

Oh, Dion, I want to say, I have long since figured out why Sunday has become our biggest hurdle. You spend nearly every Sunday with Jessie because you know I will not go anyplace with you and buy you a drink, as she will.

BUT, though screaming inside, I managed to maintain a neutral

28

attitude once he arrived back home. Imagine my surprise when, as we went to bed that night, he related to me how deep was his love, how eternal, how fulfilling. Even though he shows no outward proof of love (providing financially, putting me first, and ousting Jessie from our lives), I do believe he believes he loves me.

Monday, Dion's attempt to treat me like a lady became very evident. Several times during the day we both had to stop going in negative directions and stifle angry words that threatened to come out. He worked especially hard at calming me down (he finds my behavior as impossible as I find his). We had promised to spend the entire day together. Usually, this means nothing. However, today we actually had one day of being kind to one another ALL DAY.

There is another heartbreak about his drinking: he says when he is sober he feels nothing. I wonder if I know him at all? I certainly don't like for him to drink; yet, I do feel strange and almost uncomfortable around him when he is sober because he adopts this odd, stone-cold silence that is so unlike the Dion I know.

July 2, 19_ - Wednesday

Dion called my house around 7:00 p.m. and asked; "Are you coming over?" in that official tone of voice that lets me know Jessie is present.

I agreed to go over to his apartment. She was gone by the time I got there. He had devised yet another plan to get sober; however, within 2 to 3 hours, he was drinking Sake. Then, at midnight he left saying he was going to hand-deliver a tape to a musician. At 4:00 a.m., he came back. The outing had been an obvious opportunity to drink to oblivion, since he had emptied all available bottles in the apartment earlier in the evening.

I was so damned mad at his lack of consideration for me that I left his apartment the minute he got home. Why had I even stayed? Why had I bothered to lay awake all night listening for my van (which he took)? My own stupidity angered me as much as anything.

He clearly doesn't understand me; nor does he care. He couldn't. I'm in love with a phantom.

July 3, 19__ - Thursday

Yesterday I went back to Dion's apartment after he woke up, found that I had left during the night, and called me to come over. I went over partly because he said he has no reason to live without me; but most of all, I went over because I feel the same way. How did I escape most of my life without feeling this depth of love for anyone else that I feel for him? How can I wake up each day and, in light of all of the crap that went on the night before, still cherish him anew? What is this odd little feeling that makes me, in his presence, (despite all our problems) feel whole?

When I arrived at his apartment, I found him depressed. He continued to drink heavily throughout the day. He even managed to finagle a way to get 3 drinks out of me by saying that he needed to eat

29

something; asked me to give him money and he would drive and pick us up some food. Jessie has cut off his funds because she found out I have been spending nights at his apartment. So, I gave him money. He did need to eat. He did, however, stay gone long enough to have a few drinks.

I tried a new approach to make it through this day. I have tried to find serenity by trying to detach. I tried to listen to him today as a therapist would and not as a lover would. In doing so, I was astounded at how deeply run his feelings of self-hatred and inadequacy. This new listening helped the situation today because it helped me to resist buying into manipulations. Just for today my feelings didn't get hurt; and, we didn't fight.

Thank goodness I have been somewhat wary from the beginning about parting too easily with my money. Jessie is beginning to complain to him that she cannot pay her bills and is going to have to sell her house. Of course, I cannot help but wonder if this isn't a new form of manipulation. She appears to have lost control lately as she can clearly see that he spends less and less time with her.

Tonight, Dion admitted in a rare moment of truth that he was to blame for our fights. He said he hates this city; he longs to go back to the beach. He said he could feel himself losing control; said he didn't know how to stop it.

July 5, 19_ - Saturday

I cannot find a consistent key to getting along with Dion. I can see that he tries. And, I try. We both try so hard, but he is unaware of me so much. This morning in the midst of my frenzied attempt to make breakfast, he started hooking up all the musical instruments and asked me to practice. My priority was to eat breakfast and get to the garage sale by 9:00 a.m. (garage sales are my new way of coming up with badly needed funds). His priority was to practice music.

At first, I went along with him and we practiced for a while. But, when I stopped practicing, he got angry. Last night he procrastinated practicing so much that we never even had dinner. Finally, at midnight last night I went to bed. It's very simple. I am too tired to practice at night; he is too drunk. I am too busy to practice in the morning; he is ready to practice. Little crap like this makes our life miserable.

I have quit going to my therapist. She tries to manipulate me into giving up Dion. She says alcoholics have a character defect. Somehow, I don't buy that. She sounds like a selfrighteous, judgmental, narrow-minded, heartless......... I could go on and on. I suppose when it comes right down to it, she asked me to choose and I chose Dion.

For all of the ups and downs, I love Dion and cannot imagine life without him despite scenarios like the following: today he planned to go fishing and "dry out." He said we would be on our way as soon as he ran a "Jessie" errand (she finds more things for him to do). He ran the errand and came back home at 4:30 p.m. We still planned to go to the lake. He continued to drink and procrastinate. By 9:00 p.m., he got around to fixing dinner. With dinner in the oven, he left again for Jessie's saying he would be gone 45 minutes. One hour and 45 minutes later, he returned. I was furious. I threatened to leave.

In the meantime, Steve, the singer, showed up and tried to calm us down so he could discuss with us his new plans to represent us as our Business Manager. Steve urged Dion to play his latest song (Dion has now written 12 songs). Dion descended into morbid actions. He sang songs of love dying, etc. Then, he began to act like a Diva, threw down his $1,000 guitar in a fit of anger.

He began to write something in his daytimer as I turned to leave. When I noticed that he was headed toward the bathroom, I decided that before I left I would sneak a peek at what he had written in his daytimer. Maybe this would give me some insight into his crazed mind. He had written these cryptic words:

'As if it was God. Steve and Rose. I wonder if they will understand my silence. It's old news to me. I will speak no more except words in my music, until my songs are sold and give them the money that satisfies them. She is leaving without even a glance at me. Vow of silence.'

When Dion came out of the bathroom, I ran out the door and he followed me. But, I squealed out of the parking lot and sped home. At home, I hid my van so he wouldn't know that I was home and come bang on the door. I barricaded myself in the bedroom behind closed doors, the front door double-locked and bolted.

No, he isn't violent. I just felt the need to get far, far away. I vowed to accept no more apologies. From my vantage point, I find Dion's involvement with Jessie is nothing short of maddening; the man acts mentally ill.

July 9, 19_ - Wednesday

Monday, I drifted back into Dion's life by dropping by his apartment around 6:00 p.m. Jessie and Steve were there so he escorted me outside and we sat in my van and talked. We talked about going to an AA meeting, so I started up the engine and the next thing he knew, we were driving to the meeting. Although he didn't protest too much, it was obvious to me that he had not planned on being kidnapped and taken to an AA meeting.

We got back to the apartment at 10:30 p.m. Steve was still there; but, he said Jessie had just left. Obviously, as soon as she got home she apparently called Dion because the phone rang within 15 minutes of our being home. For some odd reason, Dion invited me to listen in on their conversation. Was I shocked to hear her ask Dion, "Is she there?"

After much delay, he said, "Yes."

Then imagine my further shock to hear her say, "What about us? It's over, isn't it?" Dion was absolutely speechless! He said, "I don't like triangles."

Then she got furious and started demanding that he return all the musical equipment, saying something like, "If you have her, you don't need me." Then she started whining about how he "never even bought her anything - not even as much as a CARD!"

I was trembling so much to hear her talk like this, so I spoke up to let her know I was listening. I said, "how long has this been going on?"

She said, in a proud and defiant tone of voice, "quite a while," (probably since May 30, when I, in yet another fit of anger and proclamation of departure, delivered him back to her house.)

I deduced for myself that Dion keeps Jessie on the string as security against my impulsive departures from his life. He even told me once that Jessie was the only constant in his life. Even I cannot argue with that. Since the beginning of our relationship, I have threatened to throw him out or leave him every other week. Therein lay some of the level of frustration between my beloved and me.

Tuesday, I watched him fight to hold onto his sobriety begun after last night's AA meeting. Jessie called every 30 minutes to an hour. Many of her desperate messages, I erased from the answering machine. Every time he deals with her, he descends into the bottle. He told me how nauseating it was to let an old woman kiss and fawn all over him in exchange for money, food, cigarettes, booze. She has apparently known all along that I threatened to leave Dion every time he began again to drink.

The thing that embroils me most is that Jessie does all the things she does in the name of Christianity. How can she ignore her tendency to call people names? She badmouths her own family. Doesn't she notice her propensity to judge all those around her who cannot further her in some way? And, why am I now judging her?

Dion says, "Jessie is not the problem; you give her too much power; she isn't very smart, etc., etc., etc."

I want to scream, "She IS the problem because she contributes to your suicide so willingly."

July 10, 19_ - Thursday

Tonight Dion and I went to another AA meeting. Tonight the subject of Step 5 came up. I was surprised to hear Dion share with the group that he had never found anyone whom he could work step 5 with. He said even when he tried to get a Catholic Priest to absolve him of this "something", the Priest said he could not. Was he referring to the man in a bar he killed in a fight? Did that really happen?

After we got back home from the AA meeting tonight, Dion answered the ringing phone and got into a huge fight with Jessie. I watched any serenity he had achieved by tonight's meeting go swiftly down the drain. When he hung up the phone he was trembling; and, I asked him what had happened. He said that Jessie had set up a 4th of July party for him to play at and he hadn't shown up, and she was still bitching about it.

I said, "Why is this the first time I have heard you speak of it?"

He put his arm around me and he said, "My Rose wasn't invited; and, I don't go anywhere anymore without my girl."

July 11, 19_ - Friday

Today Dion began to talk of wanting to take me to C_____ to visit his old home. Today was not free of its difficulties, however. Earlier in the day I had decided to try to observe rather than react. Sure enough, there were numerous attempts to twist, argue, and to manipulate. A good example of this happened during dinner.

Dion said he was starving. I suggested we go to a Mexican restaurant. He said it wasn't what he would have chosen. Sullenly, he said "but, let's go ahead." I pulled into the restaurant parking lot because he wouldn't tell me "what he would have chosen." When the waitress took our drink orders, I said I would have a coke. He ordered nothing. So, I ordered water for him. He shoved the water toward me. He said he didn't want water. The waitress took my food order. He ordered nothing. When my food arrived, I asked her to package it to go. He then decided to order food, so I asked the waitress to forget packaging my food to go and just bring me a plate. Then he ordered a beer (the whole cause of this belligerent behavior).

Had I handled this with detachment, I should have let Dion drive to the restaurant of his choice; and, I shouldn't have ordered anything for him.

Choosing not to react to his peevishness, however, I managed to pass the dinner without incident. Once home, he began to berate me for turning in the rental car and leaving him without wheels. He tried bullying me to get the van so he could drive to the Texaco. I insisted on driving him to the station.

My position as driver prompted him to complain he was in prison. I confessed I knew he only wanted to go to the Texaco to buy beer. His cover thus blown, he softened; and, we passed the evening without further incident (after he bought his beer, of course). But, even with the occasional beer, Dion doesn't drink himself into a stupor when we are together. He stays completely off the hard stuff, and, he certainly doesn't act crazy any more.

July 12, 19_ - Saturday

Jessie called Dion's apartment this morning at 7:00 a.m. Once again, after talking to her he turned white.

I could hear him say to her, "I don't think that is any of your business." Then he said, "Where did you hear that?"

I could hear her shouting because he held the phone out from his ear after a while and just hung his head.

He said, "Jessie said that she heard that I had bought you an engagement ring (true, but not technically, because although he picked out the ring, I paid for it myself). Then she said someone told her we had been married all along."

Then he said, "this has gotten completely out of hand. It's just one more thing that I don't know how to handle." He asked me to please buy us two tickets to C_____.

I said, "Dion, we can't run away."

July 13, 19_ - Sunday

Today was, all in all, a beautiful and loving day. We left the phone unplugged and actually went out together to the mall. Then we went to a car show and Dion showed me a side of himself I had never seen. He asked me to get on my knees with him; said even though I wouldn't officially marry him, would I please kneel with him and marry him before God. I said I would; and, I did.

We knelt, said silent prayers, held one another. It was a very tender moment. He looked at me with tears in his eyes and swore that he would change.

In the afternoon he said he had to go over and straighten things out with Jessie. My stomach bunched up in knots because I fear his being in her company. I have witnessed too many good intentions go right down the drain while in her company; and, I can't tell you why this happens. I don't really know their dynamics. The only thing I know about the union is that he feels sorry for her; he also feels a sense of obligation to her for all the money she has spent on him. He may push his feelings down and use people. However, he has such a soft heart that the feelings are there, underneath the surface bugging the devil out of him.

July 15, 19_ - Tuesday

Dion had been doing excellent these past few days. He seemed happy. He spent time on the phone trying to line up job prospects. He had been drinking very little. But, at 7:00 p.m. this evening, he went to Jessie's; picked up $30 and bought the stuff that makes him crazy - Schnapps.

He lied about buying it. I got so angry that he lied that I WALKED home from his apartment. So, once again, we managed to get along beautifully for only a few days. However, I am the fool here. He is obviously playing along a stupid old woman. He has no job. Talented as he is, his music suffers.

July 16, 19_ - Wednesday

Today passed fairly uneventfully. Dion, still trying to embrace some semblance of sobriety, fought having a drink until 3:00 p.m. But, something very crucial happened at 3:00 p.m. He had borrowed Jessie's car because after I walked home yesterday he said, "I don't ever want you walking again! This town is too dangerous for you to be walking places at night. If you have to leave, take your van! I'll find another way to get around."

At 3:00 p.m., knowing that he had to return her car, he stood and slugged a whole beer before he could find the courage to call her on the phone. He told her he was on the way over to return her car. At 9:30 p.m. he called from Jessie's house to ask me to come and pick him up.

34

When I picked him up, it was obvious the damage was already done. He was out of his head, falling down drunk. On the way home, I stopped and got the video SHINE.

Once home, we watched the video and Dion began to identify with the crazy man; began to fantacize that he was destined for greatness; and, acted totally nuts, whining and self-pitying until he fell asleep after babbling until 4:00 a.m.

I think Schnapps should be taken off the market. It is more than alcohol. It possesses some sort of a hallucinative property.

July 17, 19__ - Thursday

Today a girlfriend of mine called and asked me to meet her at a favorite restaurant for breakfast. I think Dion thought I was meeting another man, so he insisted on coming along. I was happy to have him though; and, at 10:00 a.m., he actually ate something.

My girlfriend invited us to come with her for the day to the mountains. We did; and, both heartily enjoyed it. It has been ages since we have gotten away and done something fun outside.

We had a beautiful day. Dion fished; we two girls swam. But, when we got home there were some strange goings on.

It started with the ringing phone; Dion answered it; it was Jessie. He hung up the phone; said Jessie had some new job prospect for him; that he was going to meet with her at the Waffle House to discuss it; he would be back within the hour.

I knew exactly where they were headed. His favorite bar is housed in the same strip mall as the Waffle House.

I decided to do something I had not up to this point, stooped to do. I would spy on them. I left his apartment, pretending I was going home. I went home alright; grabbed my binoculars; drove straight to the bar; and, parked behind some cars that hid me, yet gave me a good view with the aid of the binoculars.

In a few minutes, Jessie and Dion arrived in her car. She was all dolled up as if she was on a date. (Ironic, isn't it how fast a 70-year old Christian woman will compromise her Christian principles when necessary. One day she preaches hell fire and brimstone; predicts the demise of the latest sinner on her shit list (Steve, me, her son-in-law); the next day she goes in bars and dens of iniquity on hot dates.)

All bitterness aside, I watched them walk in together. Dion put his hands in his pockets so he wouldn't have to touch her. I think that vision of him will forever be etched on my heart. There he walked, his long blonde hair blowing in the wind; his sandals flapping against his feet; his head down; and, his hands wadded into hard balls deep within the pockets of his teal and black nylon shorts.

I sat outside the bar until 2:30 a.m., waiting for them to come out. I mainly wanted to see if he became more affectionate with her as he became more inebriated.

At one point, I had to pee, but didn't want to leave my vigil post.

Incidentally, if ever one has to "go" in an inconvenient place, here is how it is done. Hopefully, you will have had the foresight to wear a long flowing dress (as I did). Simply lift the dress, slip down panties until they are around the knees. (If you are really discrete about how you do this, people walking by will think you are just adjusting your slip.) Next, sit bare-ass naked on the sidewalk and let loose. Now, this takes a little doing. You have to watch the incline of the sidewalk and sit upstream if possible. Also, you must watch for telltale and large signs of wetness appearing on the sidewalk in front of you. Of course, at 2:30 a.m. it is sufficiently dark that most people wouldn't notice the wet cement anyway.

Well! Finally, shortly thereafter my "letting loose", the old bat comes out of the bar ALONE! I didn't even need to use my binoculars to see by her downtrodden head that her "date" wasn't going so well. She reclined alone in her car until the bar closed at 4:00 a.m. I beat it back to Dion's apartment, lay in the bed and waited to hear his "story."

Surprisingly, he was pretty truthful. Among his ramblings were thoughts about forming a band and moving to C_____ so he can support me, "his true love, his true heart." To hear him speak this way is so devastating because all I want from this man, "my true love, my true heart," is his sobriety.

July 18, 19_ - Friday

Anguished from last night's betrayal, I did something this morning that Dion hates. I got out of bed early in the morning and left his side. So many times he has begged me to sleep with him until he awakens around 1:00 p.m. For him, the 4:00 a.m. bedtime goer, that may make sense; but, for me, the early bedtime goer, the feeling of idleness and waste is so strong when I lie in bed until 1:00 p.m., that I typically spend the rest of the day feeling depressed and worthless.

I left his apartment around 7:30 a.m. and went home, knowing he would be dependent on Jessie for transportation. But, hey, it is up to him to put her in her place. It is his responsibility to get rid of her. Does he have the courage to give up all the money she gives him and find a job?

He seemed focused on finding a job earlier this month. But, his resolve became, once again, distracted by alcohol. He knows he needs to find a job. He even says he intends to find work, yet, the demons in him prove so strong that most of the time he takes the easy way out.

At midnight, after not hearing from Dion all day, he showed up at my house wanting, "his wife." Jessie had dropped him off. There is no telling what he had told her to get her to drive him to my house because she sat outside waiting like a fool for a couple of hours while he begged me to come to his apartment. I told him if he wanted "his wife," he could stay with me here at my home tonight. That is exactly what he did.

We went to bed and made love for the first time in MY bed. How could we make such beautiful love with all this turmoil between us? I

36

don't know, but we did. Afterwards, Dion said something I didn't quite understand. He said, "This is the first time in a long time that I have felt alive."

July 19, 19_ - Saturday

I knew it! She does it every time. Every time Dion tries to make it clear to Jessie that he wants to spend time with me, she "repossesses" everything.

After spending the night with me, he slept until noon; and, then we went to his apartment. Then it was that we discovered that Jessie had taken back the base guitar and the violin. She had also stopped the Texaco credit card. (She knows as well as I do that even I cannot compete with a Texaco credit card.)

So, I did as he requested and dropped him off at her house where he, no doubt, attempted to sweet talk her into returning all of his previous goodies to him. He got back to his apartment around 10:30 p.m. and called to ask if I would come and spend the night. I did.

I have many questions: what does he tell her about me? Why does she consider herself in competition with me for his affection? Why won't Jessie accept me in Dion's life if she is only the music patron? Why won't she allow him to spend time with me without putting him through hell and withholding her financial favors? I KNOW they are not intimate; but things certainly don't add up.

July 20, 19_ - Sunday

Dion and I had planned to go to church this morning, but we got up too late. Since sleeping late is so important to him, I am really trying to do so.

We played tennis and had a swim in the apartment pool. Dion had begun the day saying, "I feel like having a relaxing day."

After dipping in the pool, we went to my house where I streaked and trimmed his hair. When we got back to his apartment, there were 55 million phone messages from Jessie. It was around 4:00 p.m.; and, Dion said he had to go see her for a couple of hours.

I drove him to her house. We both could see her watching like some kind of an imbecile from the kitchen window, her shock of white hair glowing like a wild electrical current.

He wouldn't kiss me goodbye; but he looked at me and said, "It won't be much longer, I promise."

I drove back home; and, at 5:30 p.m., he called to say he was on his way back to the apartment. Asked would I meet him there so we could go to church? I waited there until 7:00 p.m.; he never showed, so I went back home.

So, my dilemma is such that if I can endure a relationship of lies (what does he tell Jessie?), missed deadlines, and a non-working partner, I can have peace. Essentially, I can maintain peace if I expect nothing.

Somewhere deep inside, Dion must surely know what is going on.

Surprisingly, his drinking is NOT his worst fault after all. Yet, I love him and truly believe he loves me through the maze. The only thing that would kill that belief is if I saw with my own eyes that he maintained any sort of a romantic fiasco with Jessie.

I think all her ridiculous jealousies are being perpetuated because a lonely old woman refuses to accept the truth. I watch her go to such lengths to obligate Dion to her with any means available to her.

Why can't I accept this reality and play along with it for Dion's sake? He has told me numerous times that she isn't very bright; she knows a lot of people; she can help his career, blah, blah, blah.

My response to him is, "maybe that is true; but, look at how much this is costing you."

Sometimes (not very often) he will hang his head and agree with me. Admitting the truth, however, has not yet evolved into embracing the truth.

I think she has discovered how easily Dion is made to feel guilty and it is my observation that she uses that button for all it is worth.

July 21, 19_ - Monday

Today was a very tense day with Steve who showed up at Dion's apartment and raged at Dion and me for wasting his time.

July 22, 19_ - Tuesday

Jessie showed up at Dion's apartment, barged right in without even knocking and stayed FOREVER.

Dion is back on the Schnapps (it makes him especially crazy). After Jessie f-i-n-a-l-l-y left, we had dinner and the evening descended into madness as Dion began to tell me every foul thing he could think of. He said I made him feel ugly. He said he couldn't make me happy. He said I forced him change so much to suit me that he didn't even know who he was anymore. He said he had lost himself. Somehow, trying desperately not to react to this venom, I endured the horror and spent the night with him. But, there were no musical recordings competed tonight. Needless to say, this was not a good day. Dion, it seems, can only be civil for 3 days; then something explodes.

July 23, 19_ - Wednesday

Dion had me drop him off at Jessie's today. Then they came back to the apartment where she stayed until 8:00 p.m. She had returned all the musical equipment she took earlier.

After she left, Dion called me to come over; but by then, the damage had been done. He hadn't eaten a thing. He had downed a pint of Schnapps. He brooded, played the music extremely loud (something he has gotten numerous written complaints for); then passed out.

I promptly left. I am so miserable; why can't I leave this situation?

Later: Lovely evening spent making love on the little sofa.

July 25, 19_ - Friday

Tomorrow is my birthday so one of my girlfriends planned a combination birthday party for her and me. Dion was invited. It was his chance to make up with my daughter and my friends who have begun to wonder if I have lost my mind. But, they accept the man I love, insanity of alcohol aside, because they know me and can see how much I love him. That's the only way I can put it.

Leading up to the party, Dion, who had borrowed, then returned Jessie's car, was stuck over at her house waiting for her to bring him back to his apartment in time for us to leave for the Birthday party. She knew we had to leave for the party at 6:00 p.m.

Finally, I called over there. When she answered, I said, "Tell Dion I am on my way over to pick him up. We are going to be late for the party."

She was very rude, saying, "I'll bring him back when I'm through talking with him," and hung up on me.

I was determined I would miss the party rather than go without him. I also decided if she thought she was causing strife between Dion and me, I would make sure she was mistaken.

Although she did bring him back late, we went on to the party where I tried to put on my best face. But, it is my only face; and, he is my only love.

July 26, 19_ - Saturday

Today, my birthday was the worst birthday of my life. My daughter had let my little grandson come home with me after the party. Dion was really enjoying the child. I had noticed when I first met Dion and he said he would like to have a child with me that he loved children. But, I had not observed him in action with a child before.

Dion bought him a toy airplane and showed him how to fly it. Then he barbecued out on the grill exactly what my little grandson requested (hot dogs and marshmallows). Also, we had plans later to go swimming in the apartment pool.

I began to tense up when Dion said he needed to make a grocery store run and asked would I give him $5.00. I gave him the money; but, I acted crappy and suspicious about doing so. Little did I know he was going to buy me a birthday card. And, what a beautiful card it was. I felt so terrible about policing him for every nickel and dime. He had obviously spent a lot of time in picking out the card because it read word for word like things he has said to me before. It read:

When a man asks a woman to be his wife,
To grow with him, to share his life,
He feels that he
Just couldn't love her more.
Yet as they share their plans
And dreams,

39

Through every phase of life it seems
His love for her
Grows deeper than before.

You are my joy,
My love, my life,
When I hold you in my arms,
I embrace everything
That matters to me
On this Earth.
Happy Birthday"

Well, as soon as we got back from the store, who should be waiting but Jessie. I went crazy.

When he parked the van, I jumped out the door and started screaming at her, "YOU COULDN'T STAY AWAY FOR ONE F_____ DAY, COULD YOU, BITCH? IT IS MY

BIRTHDAY AND YOU HAD TO F___ EVEN THAT UP WITH YOUR UGLY PRESENCE!"

Then I pointed my finger at her wishing to God it was a gun and I said, "You can HAVE him!"

By this time, Dion, in shock, had gotten out of the van. I was so crazed I didn't know WHERE I was going or what I was doing. The baby started crying. I jumped back in the driver's seat, rolled down the window and screamed one last insult, "HE'LL NEVER LOVE YOU, YOU STUPID, UGLY BITCH!" Then, I sped out of that parking lot on two wheels, praying all the time to God that I would run into a tree and kill myself.

With the baby screaming, I drove all the way to my daughter's house where I spent the night because I was trembling too much to drive home.

I suspect after I left, Dion and Jessie spent the evening conversing how horrible I am, etc., etc., etc. And, I admit it: I am horrible. I am strung tight; at the end of my rope. I am losing it.

One thing I know: he will miss me. Jessie has no leverage with me out of the picture. Dion will feel nothing but void. And, maybe just maybe with time on his hands, he will have plenty of time to remember how unfairly and how horribly he has treated me.

We had two tickets booked to go to C_____ together; but, Jessie cancelled them (so he said). Oddly enough, when she booked him a ticket she had no idea I intended to join him. But, it was his idea to get her to pay for his ticket. I had booked my own by myself. So, at this point I guess I can go alone or I can cancel the trip. I don't know; can't concentrate. I feel like I am losing it.

Around midnight I called from my daughter's house and left a terrible message on his machine. Revenge is not like me; but, I hurt so inside that I recognized I wanted only to strike back. I told him among other awful things that my daughter said he looked "lost."

He IS lost. He is more lost than any human I have ever met. I keep going back to him because I remember our good times and because underneath the addiction, we have the strongest connection I have ever felt for anyone. The connection goes both ways. In fact, Dion was the first to recognize our powerful, God-given connection. Maybe what we have between is too beautiful to be able to survive on a mortal plane. The air down here is too thin, too short on spiritual oxygen.

Then there is Jessie: so jealous of what we have that she would rather kill Dion than turn him loose. She calls herself a Christian, but all I see is an adversary, an antagonist, a controller, and a manipulator. I can see no Christian love and concern in her toward anyone? At least, that is how she appears to me. Who knows, maybe in her circles, she is a pillar of the community. Hell, if anyone were pointing to actions (and Jessie is so fond of pointing out people's "fruits"), I'm sure I resemble Satan Himself. I am sure that my actions today rivaled any exorcism movie ever written.

July 27, 19_ - Sunday

Call me crazy; but, a realization happened in the middle of the night and I see more clearly into my actions yesterday.

Dion said, and maybe correctly so, that I was trying to sabotage my own birthday. He also said that Jessie was my trigger. Of course she is my trigger! She has treated me like crap from day one. She glares daggers through me every time she sees me. I wish, oh how I WISH I could just blank her out. I MUST find a way to drop her from my soul. Otherwise, she will take not one, but two lives with her.

Dion went on to calmly note that yesterday after Jessie called; I began to LOOK for something to be wrong. Therefore, when he asked me for money to buy the card I immediately assumed: booze money, and monetary exploitation of me. That was all true. He had pinpointed my behavior with razor-sharp accuracy.

While Dion sat calmly psychoanalyzing me, I sat thinking: why can't you be so insightful in all of our dealings? Why does crisis have to enter upon the scene before you meet me halfway, Dion?

So, my new challenge rests in finding an answer to these questions: how do I stop controlling? How do I change MY destructive, character-castrating behavior? Change begins with love and trust. Do I have the strength to embrace either?

July 28, 19__ - Monday

Sunday, I went back to Dion's apartment with two gifts. I had written him a 4-page letter of apology; and, I bought him a solid gold cross to wear around his neck from this day forth.

He loved the cross and he put it around his neck with a sense of ceremony. I spent the day with him; and, talked marriage more seriously than ever before. He still depresses me because he earns no income, involves Jessie in our lives, and vice versa. Yet, on rare days such as this, when he attempts to stay sober, he is an absolute delight.

July 29, 19_ - Tuesday

I had to return to work today; and, in my absence Jessie parked herself over at Dion's apartment. In theory, leaving Dion sounds simple, but I can only accomplish this if I can go without looking at him. When I look back at him, love swells in my heart. The same is true for him. Sometimes we lock eyes and stare. Spellbound, we look at one another without saying a work. Our souls speak volumes and they do not talk the language of mortals. (I'm sure Dr. Laura would tear apart in two words every feeling I express, but she doesn't have to read this. I certainly entertain no comment from her.)

Dion's drinking interrupts his sleep. Most of the time, I end up staying up all night with him (until 4:00 a.m., his bedtime); and, I feel like I look haggard, thin, tired. I also remain especially troubled by the extent to which he goes to deny our relationship to Jessie. I know that many of their fights revolve around her demand for explanations; and, knowing him, I feel sure he is very adept at smoothing waters.

She spent all day at the apartment while I worked. When I got back to the apartment, I noticed when I went into the bedroom that Dion had hidden my nightgown. So, she obviously doesn't know I spend the nights here.

I asked Dion why he hid the nightgown. He retaliated with, "why do you act stupid? You know there is nothing going on. You know we need her to buy groceries." He said, "be patient; I am going to get on my feet."

I look at Dion these days and he looks so ill compared to our beautiful days at the beach. Back then, after only one day of being away from Jessie and her harping, questioning, booze buying, etc., he had lost that ghostly pale look and color actually came into his face. He wore a smile then; wore his hair in a ponytail. The three of us (Steve included) drove around in the van, windows rolled down, fresh salt air stinging our faces, Dion's music playing on the tape player; we singing along. Back then the three of us were intent on learning the songs Dion had written so we could go into the studio and record them. How have we slipped so far away from our dreams?

Among all the pictures we took those 10 days at the beach, we took two especially beautiful pictures. In one picture, my arms are around Dion; he is looking very adoringly at me; and, I am looking at the camera. In the other picture, I am hugging Dion closer and he is kissing my hair. We look like one person.

But, if the days seemed heaven on the beach, the nights were the third heaven. Every night we made love. We had set up the tent, a two-room nylon tent. Dion and I slept in one long rolled-out sleeping bag; and Steve slept in the van. We lit vanilla candles inside the tent; made love; and talked until 4:00 a.m. Each night we fell asleep in each other's arms. We woke the next morning the same way. I'm not sure some people have in a lifetime what we had in 10 days. At any rate, the promise of a repeat of those 10 days has carried me forth past many days like today when I feel so depressed I can barely walk into Dion's apartment. Most of my agony comes from having to stand by and to watch Dion kill himself. I am completely helpless to change him. I think I could change the tide more easily.

More often than not I want to run screaming into the streets, "Someone please help me. I have found my love, my eternal; and, there is a jealous woman who is trying to kill him so he won't be free to love me anymore. Is there no one who can help us?"

AUGUST ONE

August 5, 19_ - Tuesday

Jessie has literally moved into Dion's apartment. She stays all day every day. I don't even want to go around there. I can usually tell right away that Jessie is there when Dion calls me and speaks in that "official" tone of voice (no Honey, no Sweetie, no Baby) and asks, "are you coming over?" Usually I say, "not as long as that BITCH AND MURDERESS is there."

I know these combative actions on my part distress Dion; but his association with Jessie distresses me. I know he is caught in the middle because he literally uses Jessie to get money. But, I am caught in the middle too. I love Dion and want to work out our life together. Sometimes the problems seem insurmountable. Someone has to break the cycle. Two birds with broken wings cannot survive very long.

But, Dion scares me! He says I am not constant like Jessie. He's right. His dependence frightens me. I complain about all the money Jessie gives him, but can I afford him? He won't quit drinking. He is so insecure about me that he doesn't want me out of his sight. He won't eat. He doesn't trust me - so many problems.

When we first met, we could get along peacefully for days on end. Now, we have several fights a day. It becomes an effort to end each day on a civil note. I am convinced I am not good for him. He never knows when I am going to leave (even though all I do is run errands). And, how am I expected to commit to him totally when he maintains this separate sham with Jessie?

Sometimes I think death WOULD be a relief, and, to think that I even entertain this thought frightens me more.

On the note of death: I am prepared for Dion's death. He has lived on death's door as long as I have known him. Numerous times I have dropped to my knees and literally begged God to please let him live through this, let him live through that. Also, he is so depressed that sometimes he is downright painful to be around. Why is he depressed? Why am I scared? Why can't we be happy together? He is my world and I am his. Aren't we enough?

August 7, 19_ - Thursday

The fighting escalated into a near death experience for Dion. He admits, as he lays on his divan-death bed that he may have "gone too far this time." He says that without me, he doesn't have much reason to live. I want to scream: "and with Jessie polluting the atmosphere, I don't have much reason to live WITH YOU."

He maintains that Jessie is not our problem. He says she is his only constant and if she turns her back on him where would he go every time I threw him out. I can see his point. I can also see the vicious web we have created for ourselves. Someone needs to take charge.

Naturally, I nurse him back to health, ignoring myself, my home, my four animals.

August 8, 19___ - Friday

Dion vows to quit drinking. When I came home from work at noon, he was as near death as I've ever seen him. The Wednesday night before he had this binge, he had paged me while I was out having dinner. Of course, I went running back to the apartment only to find Jessie there. She left in a huff when I arrived. Later, she called withdrawing her support, her car, her funds (typical reaction for her when she sees me spending time with Dion). Her subliminal message is fairly obvious: "Get rid of Rose."

I always spend time with Dion, but he hides it from her. It is only when he thinks he is going to die that he seems to say, 'Screw it. I want my Rose?'

At times like these, when Rose is 'in her face,' like today, Jessie loses it. She even screamed this over her shoulder before she stormed out, "if you have her to support you, you don't need me."

Deep down she must know that Dion has me to love him and her to support him.

August 9, 19___ - Saturday

A day spent in relative quiet (for Dion, who is only quiet when he is sick). We took my grandson to McDonalds. Dion didn't feel very good, yet he enjoyed the baby so much. While I was gone taking the baby back home, Jessie visited the apartment and brought Dion groceries and money. Did I miss something! Apparently, he must have called her. Or, did she have second thoughts about her threats?

It is no secret that Jessie cannot abide Dion unless he drinks. I found this out early on when she complained about how cold he was when he wasn't drinking.

With all this turmoil spinning about around our heads, we went to bed early (10:00 p.m.).

August 10, 19___ - Sunday

I am braced for anything today. This, Dion's 4th day of sobriety, he woke moody. Initiated lovemaking, yet he seemed distant and cold. He wasn't his usual self.

Today he is reserved. I think it is called sobriety, yet even through his reserve, I can see the love light in his eyes. When pressed as to explain his mood, he said he was, "thinking about something."

I managed to get Dion to talk more about his moodiness later in the day. He said he was worried about losing the apartment; says life without me isn't living; said he didn't really feel I wanted to be with him because when couples really wanted to be together, they usually found a way. He says it grieves him that I won't marry him and "make an honest man out of him."

Oddly enough, despite the drinking, Dion is a very reverent man and devout Catholic. I have seen him practically force Jessie to take in homeless men who have just started to work. I have also seen this backfire because her benevolence appears very lopsided and leans more toward what she can get from others rather than what she can do for them.

In the afternoon, Dion was back to depending on the use of Jessie's car. As of 5:00 p.m., he has yet to come back to the apartment. Usually, she will offer to take him out to his favorite bar/restaurant so, I expect the worst.

Later: I notice the smell of alcohol. I mention this and there is bone-crushing silence the rest of the night. His silence is a combination of rage, despair, and utter desolation. I don't know how to help him.

August 12, 19_ - Tuesday

Today I did something I promised God I would never do again. I consulted a psychic.

I did it because I felt I needed direction so badly. Every circuit in my brain was receiving mixed messages about Dion and I. On the one hand, we have this great love between us. Dion himself has voiced it many times: "Honey, we are one of the greats," he said. "We are Romeo and Juliet. We are Anthony and Cleopatra." On the other hand, we are so caught up in the depth of our connection that fights become hurricanes.

So, I went to see the psychic who had advertised herself as being, '100 percent accurate.'

I took Dion's picture and as I entered her office, I was prepared to hear her say Dion and I were not good for one another. That's what everyone else had been saying. Big surprise! She surprised me by saying:

"1) He is your soul mate; 2) It would be easiest to just walk away; but, 3) God put him in your life to accomplish something; 4) God put me in Dion's life to give him the love he deserved but had never found.

She went on to say that Dion does not want to drink. Drinking is not who he is. "But," the psychic continued, " Jessie is dangerous to both of you."

She advised me to remove myself temporarily from Dion and especially from Jessie until my darkness could subside. She qualified "remove yourself from Dion" to mean "do not be sucked in Dion's manipulations and games that are inherent in alcoholic behavior." " Detach," she said.

Once back home, I attempted to apply the detachment she recommended and as a result, Dion and I spent a fairly delightful evening. I didn't interpret every dark mood as a threat. A large part of me was at work determined to nip any arguments in the bud.

Dion is extremely nervous sometimes and can be very edgy. It is best to laugh before he plunges into one of his Scottish "moods." Also, his moods are helped considerably when he just doesn't drink. He eats, he goes to bed before 4:00 a.m.

We had both been asleep for a couple of hours when, around midnight, the phone screamed into the night (Jessie). Dion didn't wake up so I unplugged the pestering phone until 7:00 a.m. this morning when he woke up.

Avoiding Jessie is like treading on eggshells. She is like the Alien. She won't go away; and, she certainly won't leave us alone. The psychic had warned me that Jessie was trying to arrange a Friday meeting with Dion. Well, this morning she called Dion and told him she had come up with all of the $594 he needed for August's rent. Then she reminded him how she never lets him down. So, he is on his way over to her house to pick up the money. I question how damaged will his heretofore 7-day sobriety become after she is finished with him? We'll see.

August 17, 19__ - Sunday

Dion began drinking Schnapps again after spending time on Thursday and Friday with Jessie.

I had left Dion money for postage because he wanted to copyright his songs that we finally got around to recording. I went on to work Thursday. In spite of my having given him the money for postage, he STILL used Jessie's charge card.

Also, I had left him the van so he wouldn't have to depend on Jessie's car to get around. But, apparently she drove her interfering butt over and spent the day while I was at work.

Although Dion was so proud of the recording work he had accomplished, I was extremely angry with him; and, I let myself become so provoked that I launched into such a temper tantrum that we became estranged again.

Saturday, despite my having the grandchildren for the day, he spent all day holed up in the apartment with Jessie parked on the divan while he pressed to get every song he had written down on tape. He even wrote a new song entitled DOESN'T IT GET TO YOU GIRL, lamenting about how the love of his life didn't love him or she wouldn't treat turn so badly.

After Jessie finally left (as she does when I come around) Dion wanted the kids to stay at his apartment so he could cook hamburgers out on the grill. But, neither of the children wanted to be around him. This hurt his feelings so deeply that even now it is difficult for me to write about it.

He is so softhearted with children. He tried to explain to the oldest Child that "Grandma and I love each other and we have a right to be together."

But, I must confess, the child cried more after hearing a strange man voice his opinion. So, I took the kids back to my home for dinner before I took them home.

After I had taken the children back home I went to Dion's apartment.

47

The experience had left him so devastated that he had cut off his long blonde hair.

He said some horrible things. He said he felt ugly. He said I had made him lose himself. He said he hated me for robbing him of his uniqueness. He said I had gotten what I wanted by making him ordinary. Said he was now finally in agreement with me that we would never make it together. In his rage and utter despair he called me horrible names. I could hear pain behind every word.

Even though he shot me hatred through his eyes and every word he uttered, he physically would not let me leave his apartment. He clung to me like a scared baby. So, I waited until he went to sleep at 4:00 a.m.; and then I left. I knew he would be devastated when he woke to find me gone. But, after all that had transpired, I was pretty shaken myself.

It is now 3:30 p.m. on Sunday and he has not called me. These times between calls every time we fight become longer and longer so I know in some important way, we are moving apart. We cannot find a way to love. Sometimes I feel I have no choice but to leave him. Even the psychic had warned to stay away for a few days. I should have listened to her.

She said we would always be together and that we had always been together. I understand this. I even feel this way. So does Dion, as evidenced by similar words spoken to me the first night I fixed him dinner.

He had looked at me across from the table that night and said, "my love for you is eternal through many husbands, many wives, many lives."

The psychic did not recommend taking the trip to C_____ that we have planned for later this month.

In my own deep frustration and anger, I called Jessie this morning. I told her that I was giving Dion up. I told her she had interfered so much in our lives that she was making it impossible for us to bond properly, that we had never been allowed to have one moments peace except that glorious week we were at the beach a million miles away from HER! I told her that all we were doing with this tug of war game with Dion was hurting him.

I compared this plight to the story of King Solomon and the two women who both claimed a certain baby was theirs. When King Solomon threatened to cut the baby in half and divide it between the two mothers, the true Mother, the one with real love in her heart said, "Give the baby to her. Don't kill it."

Of course, Jessie, ever eager to win at any battle completely ignored the implications of what I had just said. She latched onto the part of the conversation that had to do with her and said, "I never call unless he calls me. I just come by if he calls and says he needs something."

I wanted to scream at her: IF YOU ARE TRYING TO HELP SO MUCH, WHY WON'T YOU ACCEPT ME! WHY DO YOU HAVE TO BATTLE ME?

But, even as I think these thoughts, I know that much of the responsibility for rectifying this mess rests upon Dion himself. Until he quits drinking and gets honest, we haven't a chance. So, right now I feel I must give up. I resolve not to return his phone calls.

August 18, 19__ - Monday

Away from Dion, I went to work. He called my pager several times. He is devastated. He doesn't seem to understand the havoc he wrecks. Weakening, I went to his apartment to listen to him vent his frustration. Every story has its version and Dion's version makes ME Sound like the bad guy.

It is very obvious. We are all on this destructive merry-go-round. Dion drinks; acts irrational; I react; aggravate him; act like someone who hates him when really, I adore him with all my heart; he reacts in anger, rejection; I leave; he grieves; drinks to dull the pain; and on and on. When he finally approaches death and we both realize how much we stand to lose, he attempts sobriety.

Enter Jessie, who, after a few days of not hearing from him (he never calls her when he attempts to quit drinking), calls every 30 minutes until we are either forced to answer or take the phone off the hook. Then sometimes that doesn't even stop her. Oftentimes, she will drive over and bang on the door until we are forced to answer.

I want us to get help, but am I going to Al Anon, as I should be? No. Dion refuses therapy. I know the drill. I should go on to therapy by myself, but I don't.

August 19, 19__ - Tuesday

Without the benefit of sitting down and having a deep heart-to-heart talk, I tried spending the night at Dions apartment. But, unable to sleep because or repressed anger, I left in the middle of the night (knowing this would piss him off). I seem to be just trying to aggravate him. It feels like my anger has nowhere to go. I kid myself that I can deal with it myself. O obviously I cannot. We need desparately to sit and quietly communicate. All that really happens is that I bottle up my anger and it becomes expressed in mean little passively destructive ways. Maybe this is why Jessie hates me.

August 20, 19__ - Wednesday

Dion and I attempted to record some music for our agent through this thick haze of smothered anger. We kept getting into fights and nothing got accomplished. He had asked me to drive him over to Jessie's. I know his tension is because he wants a drink.

I drove him over to Jessie's. Although he expected to just run in and get some money or whatever, I was so angry I just drove off and left him stranded there. I didn't even care at this point if he spent the night there. (Guess she has to drive him home.)

August 21, 19__ - Thursday

The results of my destructive actions left Dion nearly unconscious. He apparently drank so much that they called the ambulance and now he is back in the hospital in intensive care.

August 22, 19__ - Friday

This is Dion's second day in intensive care. He hangs on, but he is very damaged. Meanwhile, the lease on his apartment has been cancelled. I went by there last night and found a note on the door that said, "due to a complaint of loud music playing late at night"......... they were canceling his lease as of the end of this month.   Now, I am faced with a brand new decision.

Do I let Jessie move him back to her house, as she has been begging and I have been threatening? Or, do I take it upon myself to move his things over to my house?

I know were he to move back in with Jessie, he would surely die. I also have this deep sense that in a way Jessie WANTS Dion to die. In a sick way, she would rather see him die than see him be happy with me. She keeps saying crap like "He'd be better off with the Lord."

Many times Dion has commented, "If I don't have my gal by my side, I don't have any reason to go on."

Once, on one of those rare occasions when he and I engaged in true communication rather than cheap fighting, he said to me that he had lost all faith in humanity until he met me. He said that I gave him hope; made him want to fight and to live.

He wrote the song *LIFELINE* for me. The lyrics say:
"...........there still are heros riding hard
while they travel across the deserts.
There's still a steal in their eyes
As they ride against the winds.
And, they never stop to sleep
Not even in the darkness
Until the promises they made
Let them come to rest at last."

He once explained that he never went to sleep before 4:00 a.m. because he was, to quote the song lyric, "never stopping to rest until the promises he made to me were complete."

And, never let it be said that he hadn't promised to take care of me. He did make that promise. I could see that in his own way, he was trying. He truly was doing the best he could (under the circumstances).

So, regarding my decision whether to throw him to the wind or move him in with me was pretty much a foregone conclusion. He was so unhappy around Jessie that he drank ten times as much as when he was away from her. And, if it was true when he said he needed me; that he couldn't make it without me, I couldn't just drop him into the pit.

August 23, 19__ - Saturday

Dion's third day in Intensive Care finds him recovering more slowly than usual. He is yellow; his stomach is still swollen; his urine is deep orange, etc.

They say you really don't know how much you love someone until they aren't there anymore. This truth was driven home to me time after time when I actually faced losing him. Every emotion between us seemed heightened. I came to the hospital today with a heavy heart because I don't know how to love this guy. He thinks he can't make me happy; and, I don't know how to make him happy. He entered my life so damaged already. Sometimes I think he was born under an unlucky star and instead being allowed the peace that death brings, he was so strong that he persevered. Only, his soul seems to have died.

During my visit to the hospital, we remained very cautions in our conversation. In a sober state, he reveals a much more sensitive side than one would ever suspect. However, he has his own strong opinions. For instance, don't even suggest what he SHOULD do. Also, he hates gossip or any talk about other people (Jessie).

Jessie called to tell me she would move the musical instruments back to her house. When I told him this, he got upset. Yet, when I offered to move his clothes to my house, he didn't want to discuss that either.

So, with exactly a week left to vacate the apartment, he won't say what are his wishes or intentions.

We are best when we stick to words of love. We are best to try laughter. Other stuff finds him out or sorts in two seconds.

August 24, 19__ - Sunday

Dion's condition this forth day in Intensive Care is a little better. When I was there yesterday he looked at me with a very serious look in his eye. He said, "Do you love me?"

I said, "More than life itself."

He said, "I gotta have a reason to fight, you know."

I started to bring up Jessie and tell him I wish he would get her out of our life, but I decided to speak no negative words. He then took my hand and said, "Without my gal, I don't see much reason to go on."

I said, "Well, you've got me. Heart and soul, you've got me."

He is off intravenous food; he is eating solid food and sleeping a lot.

August 25, 19_ - Monday

Was I shocked when I went to the hospital today. Dion's condition worsened in the night and when I went into the room, I found him with an oxygen mask! Seems his blood pressure had dropped from a reaction to the water retention medicine they prescribed for him.

I went straight home; got down on my knees and begged God to please let him live. I promised God that I would begin to tithe. (One of God's laws I find especially difficult to do.)

August 27, 19__ - Wednesday

I made a gutsy decision and moved Dion's stuff into my place. I figure things with him can only go two ways: 1) if he continues to drink, he will die; 2) he may quit drinking. In that case, I love him and I will definitely marry him.

August 28, 19_ - Thursday

For some reason, the doctors let Dion come home today. I almost feel they released him to "go home to die." However, they underestimate the will of this man. He will fight death to the end. Many times he has told me that he had lost his will to live until he met me. He has said (and I believe him) that I give him a reason to live. He said he regretted that he didn't anticipate his life turning out to be worth something after all. He expressed regret that he didn't take better care of his health before we met. I have assured him that if only he will quit drinking, we can still have quality of life.

Tonight at home was very touch-and-go, as he spent much of the time very weak and in pain.

August 29, 19__ - Friday

Suddenly, after dinner, Dion perked up. He still has dark circles under his eyes. He still has a swollen belly from the badly diseased liver and the nearly absent pancreas, but he has improved.

Jessie is fighting us to get his stuff back over to her house. She calls me and tells me all sorts of slanderous things about him. However, something tells me she is just trying to make me want to let him go. She mistakenly thinks if I would just go away, she could "have" him. She conveniently ignores how he tries to drink himself to death every time I DO leave the scene. She is too ignorant to realize he will never love her.

When she called today to try to get back the musical equipment and to suggest that we do the recordings at her house, Dion said, "she doesn't care about my health. She just doesn't want me living with you."

I said, "she wants the musical equipment back."

He said, "she is just manipulating us."

I didn't tell Dion how she had outdone herself by suddenly pretending to be my friend so she could confide all these awful things that she had to say about him.

She called one day out of the blue to gossip about negative comments supposedly leveled by various members of Dion's family: as reportedly said by his son, "he is an embarrassment to the family." As reportedly said by his Stepfather, "The best thing you can do is get away from him before he drags you down." As reportedly said by his sisters, "we don't want anything to do with him."

But, listening to my heart and walking by faith, I have defied everyone else who has offered me advice, why should I suddenly start listening to a woman who has heretofore HATED me, who now pretends to be my friend; and, who says, essentially: 'Dion is bad. Move him out. Move him in with me.'

My soul knows (the same soul that knows that Dion is my eternal other, given to me by God) that Dion will commit a slow chemical suicide if I turn my back on him - he has made a pretty good dent in it so

52

far.

He said to me tonight, "If I survive this, I promise to make you a good husband." I believe him.

SEPTEMBER ONE

September 1, 19___ - Monday

Dion and I watched a special on Andy Gibb that left me with cold chills. There are so many similarities. Dion LOOKS so much like an older Andy Gibb that I sat and looked at the TV, then looked at Dion. Both men are (were in the case of Andy) born under the sign of Pieces. Both have very kind, sweet, sensitive personalities (rendered complete opposites by their addictions). Both are (were) musicians. Even Andy's love of his life, Victoria Principal, looks like ME. Also, she was older than Andy, as I am older than Dion. But, the most troubling similarity: every loved one and friend in Andy's life stood hopelessly by watching him die before their very eyes. No one could find a way to help him. Needless to say, he verified their fears by dying at the young age of 30. Dion is 46; and, thank God he is still with me.

This is Dion's 12th day of sobriety. He has been easy to live with until today when after putting off since Friday Jessie's insistence to "repossess" the musical equipment, he finally agreed today to meet with her.

Well, she called today and within seconds of hearing her voice, he became a changed man. He descended into a dark hole where not an ounce of light could be seen. His eyes took on that odd dead look; and now he is as silent as death.

After the conversation, he fought to find an argument with me. He seemed to be trying to uncover insults and slights in everything I said to him. For instance, we were supposed to go fishing today. I kept waiting for him to get ready, waited for him to fix his fishing pole. I resisted asking, "Are you ready?" because I didn't want him to crowd him, but finally around 3:30, I could wait no longer. I said, "Dion, I am ready to go when you are."

He said in a very vexed tone of voice: "It's 3:30. We can't go now; it's too late in the day." Then he sat back on the divan and just stared into space. It is in times like these that I ask myself:

1) What ever convinced me there was love here?

2) Where is the passion he once had? Is this what sobriety should look like?

3) Why did this man so diligently destroy my relationship with the boyfriend? Just to sit and stare into space and withdraw from me? For what reason does he behave thus? Is it because he had some words with Jessie?

4) How could I have been so stupid to move him in with me? What ever made me think things would work out?

5) What has blinded me so? (I know the answer to this. I love this man.)

So, now here I sit in my own home, having moved Dion in and I feel miserable when he gets in these moods. I also feel trapped in my own home by this monster named Jessie who continues to barge in and cloud the air between us.

Another troubling thing: there is a blackness that torments Dion. If my spiritual eyes were only stronger, I would be able to see this terror that follows him. In his presence, I often feel a powerfully tormenting sense of doom. His despair is almost painful. Sometimes just to leave the room provides me with a feeling of relief. I fear if I could see with spiritual eyes, I would see black, smelly demons attached like leaches to every ounce of his flesh. I am scared and don't know how to address this ambiguity. Although it sounds somewhat foolish, I often contemplate asking a Priest to perform an exorcism. Do they still do that?

I KNOW this is not my imagination because one night the cat noticed it too. He climbed up in the swivel chair, stared at the ceiling and began to howl in this long, mournful voice.

Dion seemed panicked. He said, "I once had a cat who acted this way before my father died. He acts like he sees the angel of death who has come for someone."

I said, "DION, DON'T SAY THAT!"

September 4, 19__ - Thursday

Like the wind, Dion's mood changed again shortly after the horrible Monday. In my presence alone, without any input from Jessie (we have taken to ignoring her phone calls all day long--sometimes I just unplug the phone for the day), he becomes calm again. Often I sense that Dion is as frightened as I am. We both totter on eggshells. We experience this wonderful depth of love; yet, we feel it being threatened also. I'm not sure either of us can effectively name the enemy.

Yesterday, we went fishing and we spent the day outdoors. That seemed to help his mood more than anything. Last night he actually confessed to having been difficult. He claimed complete responsibility for our problems. He said he felt ashamed about being sick and not able to contribute to our finances. He says he NEEDS to work; he wants to work; he feels useless without work. However, work, to date, has meant dealing with Jessie and we both know THAT has been a dismal failure.

He confessed that Jessie wants to keep us apart so he will be with her. That, I had already surmised; but, when I say these things, he becomes extremely belligerent. So, I have tried especially hard since he has come home from the hospital and has maintained his sobriety not to even MENTION her.

He said, "Rose, you are the only human I don't move around like a pawn. That is because I love you."

September 5, 19__ - Friday

Dion slept on the couch because his poor stomach hurts. It sticks way out. We measured and he measures 35 1/2" around the abdomen. The swelling is due to the ascites condition. Although he is in intense pain, he asked me to lie down with him on the couch and just hold him.

At 2:30 pm the phone rang (Jessie home from work); but we ignored it. Shortly thereafter, we got up and left for the acupuncturist.

Driving home, he decided he wanted to stop and get hotdogs. I am broke and thought he wanted me to charge groceries. Very unhappily, I walked into the grocery store. He paid for the hotdogs; but, sensing my depression, he lapsed into the ice-cold, stone-shoulder routine once we got home. This time, I was wrong here. I shouldn't be so paranoid about money. This is especially true since I see how hard he is trying to absent himself from Jessie and her financial dole.

Fixing his own hotdog, he ate reading a book. I know my tension over money started this cold war. I ask myself why can't we rise above this pettiness once and for all?

September 6, 19__ - Saturday

Yesterday's tension over money set Dion off to go to Jessie to ask her to buy groceries. He got home around 9:00 p.m. I tried not to react to the late hour; and, things actually went smooth whereas once upon a time this would have been a launching pad for a huge fight.

Truth is, I feel responsible for this latest trip to Jessie's to get money. On the one hand I ask him to oust her from our life knowing full well that he has no visible means of support other than her handouts. As if that weren't painful enough for him to face, I threaten to squeeze a dime with my stingy ways so that he feels trapped with more to worry about than just his swollen belly and his fight with sobriety. This disease is such a frightful maze.

September 7, 19_ - Sunday

Dion is being stronger than I would have ever given him credit for. Whereas once upon a time the tension over money would have thrown him into a tailspin, he has recovered from any hurt feelings.

We went to the lake today and had lovely fishing. We took guitars and played and sang songs until night fell. He taught me some new chords and we vowed to rehearse and learn two new songs a week. After all, our original plans were to play and sing together.

Tonight Dion wrote and sang to me the sweetest song he had written. It said something like, "of all the women he had known, I was his "true heart." The song went on to lament as to how he had taken care of all those other women so why wasn't he taking care of me? It also said that all I ever asked from him was love; yet, how I deserved so much more; and, how he vowed to take care of me.

I became encouraged by the song lyrics because it sounded like a vow of recommitment and rehabilitation. This is another area where I feel I have failed Dion. He is so passionate about his music. He loves my voice and has tried numerous times to involve me in active rehearsals and musical commitments. However, I always seem to have housework or other work that comes first. Oftentimes, the noise from the powerful speakers is an issue because we seem to have this wealth of complaining neighbors.

The universe appears to conspire against Dion. Everywhere he turns, he seems to be fraught by opposition of some sort. I swear, someone out there has it in for him.

September 12, 19__ - Friday

Dion went to the hospital for a follow-up check. He was in such bad health that they kept him. They checked him in there on the spot. No wonder he has been feeling so badly. He should have never been released in the first place. All along, I had had this strong feeling that they just sent him home to die. SURPRISE! He didn't die.

His blood pressure was too low to do the GI work; and, his ascites was so bad they were afraid he had developed an infection. This explains why he has been difficult; he didn't feel good even though he was trying so hard to get well - and that included a commitment to sobriety.

September 16, 19__ - Tuesday

I have sat with Dion every night at the hospital. He is such a delight when sober. I don't think I have realized how many of his bad moods had to do with pain and suffering, the side effects of end-stage Cirrhosis.

Since he is still in the hospital, I realize he was obviously dangerously ill when he was home. I miss so much having him home. Funny how I never realize how empty I feel until he isn't around. Talk about taking someone for granted. He fills up a void I didn't even know was there until he came into my life. I always attempted to fill my void with work or with shopping.

One of our ongoing arguments has been that Dion says that I only focus on the negative aspects of our relationship. This is probably true. I must be somewhat of a perfectionist in that I don't allow myself to admit happiness unless everything is by-the-Barbie-Book perfect. I think they call this: not counting your blessings.

I fear for his health. The ascites has begun to accumulate in his genitals. This is pretty unusual, I think. The medical books say his only hope for survival at this point is a transplant. He continues to fight for his life (he is SUCH a good soldier); but, he looks bad.

I love him so much that often I get angry at having missed a normal life with him: a life with kids and church.

He was the first one to bring up having children. He looked at me one night in a restaurant and said, "I would love for us to have a child. What a beautiful child that would be." He looked so handsome that night: twinkle in his eye, shoulder-length blonde hair.

I had a faith healer come to the hospital today to lay hands on Dion's stomach. Although it was solely my idea, he went along with it. But, I could tell by the look in his eyes that he felt foolish and ganged up on.

I could feel a healing spirit moving all around us as the two of us lay hands on him. I began to cry. Dion tried to look his most dead with an almost angry cast to his eye. Once during the session after apparently noticing the same angry expression, the faith healer asked him what he was thinking. He happened to be looking at me when he answered, "I'm thinking how beautiful my Rose is." You could have fooled me.

Later in talking to the healer I asked her if she thought Dion loved me. She thought for a minute; then she said, "I can tell he loves you because his eyes change when he talks about you."

September 20, 19__ - Saturday

The faith healer had taken me aside on Wednesday and asked me to make an appointment to see her. So, I had scheduled the appointment for today.

I went to her house for an hour-long meeting, which vaguely resembled a therapy session. She expressed concern that I was all love and Dion was in such psychic pain. She warned me that he WOULD drink again. She said his eyes were dead. She said there are a lot of feelings he has yet to deal with. These were things I didn't want to hear, but I listened anyway. She said although he has a few weeks of sobriety, it should only be considered as detoxification; that true sobriety needs at least 6 months duration to even approach definition. Then, she gave me this odd warning, "Love yourself. Don't even burden him by looking to him for love."

Admittedly, it has been difficult to be near a man who does little these days but read cookbooks (his interest in food has replaced his interest in alcohol). But, he is trying. Why am I complaining? Could it be I am "looking to him for love?"

September 21, 19_ - Sunday

Evidently the faith healer healed Dion's liver because he began to improve steadily from that day on until he was finally able to come home last night.

Today has been a very tense day as I try to have fun around an unusually cold, undemonstrative stranger! However, forewarned by the healer, I strive to be patient and to give him time. Also, I must give myself time to adjust to the "sober" Dion. This is what I wanted wasn't it? How much of his distance is old anger?

I have so many unanswered questions that I should be in some kind of recovery myself. I know this, yet I continue to behave in the same old manner. Daily I move away from the healer's words when she warned, "love yourself. Don't look to him."

September 23, 19__ - Tuesday

Gradually each day, Dion's tenseness has softened. Our lovemaking returns to its original steam with the huge belly gone. But, Dion went to Jessie's at 4:00 p.m. saying he had to get back to work. That he was tired of lying around. I begged him to just give himself time. Begged him to get well first, then look for work. But, he doesn't listen to me.

He came home at 11:00; but, thank God, he hadn't had a drink. He is beginning to look so good. He has even begun to put on weight (something very difficult to do with a diseased liver). But, something has been bothering him and he answered it tonight by saying, "Please marry me. It is time to either marry or get off the pot."

September 26, 19__ - Friday

This week has been a fog for me. Each day is tension-filled as I struggle to keep peace between us; and, as Dion struggles to resist alcohol.

When I got home from work at 4:00, he was gone. I'm sure Jessie picked him up. I was so distraught that I went to the drugstore, bought Valerian, came home, took two and lay down and began to read a male-female dynamics book called MARS AND VENUS ON A DATE.

Although the book was quite an eye-opener, I do believe most of our dysfunction has more to do with alcohol than with our male-female dynamics. Dion always says we are great together. He says I focus on the negatives.

However, I seem to do a lot of things wrong according to the book. For instance, I tend to pay attention to HIS needs instead of to ask him for help (which, supposedly, makes a man feel more like a man). Okay, so I do too much for him and should, instead, ask for his help. This must be something Jessie knows because she has Dion do EVERYTHING for her.

Anyway, he arrived at 8:30 p.m. (still sober, thank God); and, I immediately applied some lessons I had learned in my crash course, and he DID warm up. He said he had been missing me; we lay down on the couch and cuddled; he began light kisses on my neck.

September 27, 19_ - Saturday

Dion and I have gotten along beautifully for days. As usual, Jessie threatens to ruin it by withholding the $100 she so manipulatively dangled in front of Dion to get him over to her house to fix her damn car. Now it is 3:00 p.m.; we had planned to go to the Greek Festival or the movies or anything; and, she isn't home to pay Dion. My guess is that she will come dragging in late this evening just to keep him there; keep him through dinnertime; then suggest they go to dinner at one of his favorite dives; we will have lost a weekend day; and, Dion will have lost his sobriety.

In an effort to get Dion to stay home, I say, "I have $50. Please, let's go out and do something. You can collect from her another day."

He answers me by saying that he doesn't want to take money from me. Out the door he goes.

Dion came back home at 9:30 p.m.; and, as I feared, he had broken his 36-day sobriety. I am so disappointed that I don't even care to work on the relationship anymore. I am so angry I don't feel anything anymore. Don't feel love, don't feel hope, don't feel sad. I feel numb and defeated. He is sick right now from having drunk however much he drank; and, I am so angry I don't care. I have tried SO HARD to make this work. But, nothing I do makes any difference.

September 28, 19__ - Sunday

Today is a day of INCREDIBLE silent treatment from Dion. He is, of course, reacting to my silent treatment last night when I crept off the divan and went to bed (we had fallen asleep on the divan).

This morning he cried and says he doesn't know what to do about us. He reasons that I am very unhappy with him; doesn't think I like him; doesn't think I am happy. I keep thinking: 'if only you would change;' and, he keeps thinking: 'if only you would change.'

Obviously, the only thing we have going for us is this phenomenal chemistry, which when it is bad it can be very, very bad. There is so much tension between us as both of us are afraid of messing things up. There is even new tension in our lovemaking, which used to be so spontaneous and tension-free. He is right. I am miserable. So, why can't I say, "Go ahead. Move out!"

I feel a big ball of uncried tears in the center of my chest where my heart is. I know from whence comes the expression 'broken heart'. It feels exactly as if my heart is breaking in two. All the formulas for how to get along with men are going right out the window because the woman is supposed to act happy so the man can feel good like he is making her happy. But, all I want is for Dion to hold me like he used to do before we moved in together.

Back then, he would call me when he was ready to see me and what little time we spent together was so concentrated it just seemed like a lot. Being around him now sometimes feels like a slap in the face, especially when he decides to put on his cold shoulder or sullen face. Of course, I know what is happening. He is in a tense state of sobriety; and, is, at the same time, suffering disappointment at my refusal to marry him.

He said once, with tears in his eyes, that I needed to "make an honest man out of him." Oddly enough, I think he really does feel that way.

September 30, 19__ - Tuesday

Last night Dion dropped me off at church where I am taking classes to join so we can be married in the church. Although we had had a lovely day of no alcohol, I had the old nagging fear that he wanted the van to go get a drink (because he has been drinking off and on since his Saturday sojourn with Jessie).

He picked me up after church and it was obvious that he had made a special effort to get dressed up and look nice. In fact, he looked gorgeous in suit and tie. He seemed determined for us to have an enjoyable evening. But, at the first whiff of alcohol, I was off and running; completely lost my cool; told him he would have to leave.

We ended up salvaging the evening somehow by sheer effort on both of our parts. But, the blatant truth is that neither of us will give the other the thing most important. Most important to me is he NOT DRINK. Most important to him is I accept him as he is, including his "one flaw" (as he so often puts it).

This morning a change arrived in my heart. I realized that no matter

60

how loosely I have thrown around the word "love," I have not practiced unconditional love. I have expected and demanded that Dion CHANGE before I would accept and marry him. At the same time, he remains tense and unhappy because I won't marry him.

The facts are this: Dion is an alcoholic I knew this when I met him. But, I went ahead and got involved with him and then demanded that the rules be changed.

I have reached this conclusion: I love Dion too much to leave him. Call me foolish; but, even as I say this, I also know that God intended this union. He put us together for a reason. I believe that this is the man God intended from the beginning of time for me to marry. Further, I believe we will be together for eternity. Dion must believe this also because on our first date he said, "My love for you is eternal."

My prayer is a new one. My prayer is for God's Perfect Will to be done. As for love, there is no turning back for me. But, I must find a way to accept the whole man. I love him so much that acceptance must be a foregone conclusion.

OCTOBER ONE

October 1, 19__ - Tuesday

Although I was able to get through the entire day and night without resenting Dion's light drinking, I still have much tension over trying to maintain my new attitude without the benefit of Al Anon meetings. Why won't I commit to those meetings! One thing is time. Dion complains when I spend time away from him. He acts like a man who knows he has almost run out of time and is attempting to make up for lost time. I've begged him to come with me. Let's go to an AA meeting together, I say. But, he thinks meetings are copouts. Thinks they are "a bunch of whiners talking about themselves all the time."

October 2, 19__ - Wednesday

We have begun to communicate better. He attempts to explain his moodiness, his coldness. He says he is afraid to love me; afraid I will die (huh?). He also says he is unable to forget some of the harsh words I have said to him. They haunt him, he says. He is referring to horrid things I have said in exasperation like, "I am miserable;" or "let's end this;" or "this was a mistake;" or "get out of here;" - all that crap.

In my own defense, I can only say I have NEVER experienced such strong emotions for anyone before. Those emotions run as bad as they do well. They are much heightened. Lately I have asked myself how I could have come this far in life without feeling anything. Have I gone through most of my life not feeling?

Jessie has started demanding much of his time again. She keeps coming up with different business ideas for them to embark upon together. She calls all the time; and, admittedly, he spends most of our waking time with her. It is 4:30 p.m. and he is with her in my van. I have her car. It is crazy.

October 4, 19__ - Friday

I learned the reason Dion had taken Jessie in our van. He was attempting to get her to buy new tires for the van. Lately, he has been asking me to, "please lets get away to the ocean and renew our love." There is a song with lyrics something like, "let's go to the water and try." Dion turned it up loud on the radio one day while we were driving in the van and just sort of smiled that hazy smile of his that says he knows I am reading his mind.

Dion does love the ocean. He is a different man while there. I've never experienced such joy as that all too brief time we spent near the ocean, but work keeps me so tied down.

He wants to move to the water. How tempting it would be to move away from Jessie. It is also a consideration for Dion's health. I never saw him look so well and drink so little than our brief times spent near the water.

October 6, 19_ - Sunday

A wonderful day of lovemaking. Surprisingly, Dion spent today with only me! I always know he is determined to quit drinking when he spends Sunday with me because he can't buy alcohol in the stores on Sundays; and, he KNOWS I won't take him to a restaurant and buy a drink. Usually, the only way he can manage to have a drink on Sundays is to hang around Jessie.

We also played tennis, but his energy was low. Yet, he talks like he is determined to build back his health, his strength, and his atrophied muscles. I can see that he is trying.

October 7, 19__ - Monday

Something happened to Dion's spirit during the time I was at work today. When he picked me up from work, he was acting very needy. Example: "hold me, cuddle me," etc.

I went to bed at 10:00 p.m. He left in the van and returned at 2:00 p.m. He talked great words of love; but, physically, he was in much pain.

October 8, 19_ - Tuesday

As things get better between Dion and I, I find I don't write about them. I only turn to the diary when I am in psychic agony.

It became obvious to me today that Dion planned the usual outing with Jessie because after ignoring numerous phone calls from her, he began at 5:00 p.m., to feign concern for the van. Then at 6:30 p.m., he called her, asked her to meet him at Ace Hardware to buy some things to fix the van.

We had tentatively planned to go to the movies at 7:30. I knew that would never happen because at 5 minutes to 7:00 he still hadn't walked out the door. I said, "do you really think you will make it to Ace Hardware by 7:00, do what you need to do and get back here in time for the 7:30 movie?"

He said with some remorse, "I hate to leave you."

I knew then that the two of them had made previous plans.

Dion came home at 8:00 p.m. SURPRISE! We went out to eat. While we were eating, the waitress came up to Dion as if she recognized him. She said, "that lady you were with left her jacket."

It then became obvious to me that he had just left this same restaurant with Jessie. They probably had previous plans to eat here. He got to the restaurant, began to feel guilty, picked an argument; they left in a huff; and, she forgot her jacket.

Naturally, I became furious. Naturally, we fought. Naturally, once at home I pouted, gave him the cold shoulder; and naturally, he called her. I was so CRAZED I listened in on the conversation.

She flirted unmercifully with him. She said, "I wish I had a big plot of land. I would take everyone I loved there."

I could have died. Then, he said they needed to take a vacation.

Needless to say, my heart is broken. But, he denies having done or said anything wrong. Makes me look like the untrusting bitch.

He sat me down, stared at me like he was trying to hypnotize me and he said, "Why do you let Jessie trigger you? You know there is nothing between us."

I said, "SHE seems to think there is."

He said, "That's her problem." Then he said, "If I was going to cheat on you, it wouldn't be with some gray headed old woman twice my age. I would find some beautiful young thing."

Then he went on to say, "In many ways, Jessie is my best friend. She makes me feel important. She believes in me. She likes the music. You hate the music."

I said, "Dion, I don't hate the music."

All he said to that was, "Didn't you notice that I took away the music?"

As a matter of fact, he has stopped playing music anywhere in the house. This makes me feel oddly out of touch with Dion. Maybe I haven't been doing a very good job of "seeing" him. Maybe I am focused too much on myself. Obviously, if I had been sensitive about tonight, I would have realized that Dion started the evening out with plans with Jessie; got to the restaurant; had a change of heart; and, came back for me. That acknowledgement by me might have aborted this huge fight.

October 9, 19__ - Wednesday

While I worked, Dion spent the day at Jessie's. It is now 9:00 p.m.; and, I must say, I give up. I called this Prophet of God (so she calls herself); and talked with her about my problems.

She said I appeared helpless; said I should pray that God heals Dion's emotions; that He restore Divine Order; that He send Jessie back into the universe. In a strange way, her words made perfect sense to my troubled heart.

Earlier in the night, Dion called. I expressed despair and frustration because I could tell he was drinking heavily. So, it is now 9:00 p.m.; and, I am going to bed. I don't care. I feel like giving up. I might as well accept that he would probably spend the rest of the week with the murderess. We cannot build any kind of relationship with this mess of a merry-go-round. In fact, it is obvious that we need a marriage counselor. Or do we? Or don't we? Of course we do.

Dion is not "doing unto others" as he would have "others do unto him." I guarantee you, if I spent all this time with another man, he would be pissed. He even admitted it one night, quietly announcing to himself, "Time to get rid of the other woman."

By Thursday, I was so damned angry at Dion that we escalated into a fight that ended up at Jessie's where she played the innocent; and, I demanded he move back in with her.

I left him there, but he ended up back at home at 2:00 a.m. with liver problems. I told Jessie, "Let him die. That's what he wants."

October 10, 19_ - Thursday

With some relief to be away from Dion, I went straight from work to my daughter's house to baby-sit. In the back of my mind I had intended to bring the kids home with me; but Dion stayed out until midnight with Jessie so I'm glad I stayed over at my daughter's.

He said he had been paging me all night; but, I had fallen asleep at 9:00 p.m. Finally, at 2:00 a.m., my pager woke me up; I called home and talked to him. He said he missed me.

October 12, 19__ - Saturday

After being gone from home during the morning, I arrived at 11:00 a.m. just in time to meet Jessie waiting for Dion in her car. She sheepishly mentioned that Dion wanted to go get art supplies and start working on the "business" project they planned to do together.

He was shocked to see me; thought I would be gone until 3:00. He told her to wait in the car; then he kept her waiting there so long that she finally left.

But, he jumped in the van and went running after her. It is 9:45 p.m. and he is still over there. He has called twice. Said he worked on the van tie rods.

He admits Jessie hates me and doesn't want us to be together. That's pretty obvious. She certainly stays busy dogging him with the constant ringing of the phone those few placid moments that we do manage to have together, those few fires we manage to enjoy by the fireplace, those few games of tennis we get to play.

His Jessie thing usually starts with him going over there so she will buy him something - clothes, tools, cellular phones, books, CD's, alcohol, cigarettes - anything he wants. This works very effectively at keeping him away from me; because, by the time he DOES return home, he is so wasted I don't even want to be around him.

I am furious at Jessie and at God for allowing this self-righteous Christian to manipulate not only my man, but also our love relationship. Yes, I am helpless. You betcha. Dion earns no income; and, when he looks to me to support him the way she does, I can't. I can barely support myself.

Meanwhile, all the progress made healthwise is being reversed as he drinks steadily and heavily while in her company. I've seen her serve him alcohol; whereas, he has a difficult time in my presence even saying the word. I am so angry I could scream. When we finally do get together, I am so angry I can't be civil and things descend into screaming fits.

October 13, 19__ - Sunday

Dion came home last night at 11:00 p.m.; said he had worked on the van (he can't work on our car at our home because Jessie "repossessed" the tools - he has to "work" over there). It was obvious that he had been working on the van because he had grease all over him.

Today, I thought we were having a perfectly good Sunday. He had promised me he would spend the entire day with me. He kept making trips to the car, each time coming back smelling of beer.

Anyway, we had a long heart to heart talk, which perhaps made him comfortable enough to ask me to go have a beer with him. I refused. I will not support any part of this habit that kills him.

When I refused, he accused me of forcing him over to Jessie's (which I recognize as manipulative talk). He said, "But I would rather be with you I was hoping we could have a pleasant evening; but, you are sending me out."

Dion, you really outdid yourself this time.

I put back into the refrigerator the meat thawed for tonight because although it is 5:00 p.m., after he is through with the white-haired murdering bitch, it will be midnight.

We have a C_____ trip planned beginning Saturday; and, plans are still on to go. However, if he continues to drink, he won't live to go.

October 15, 19__ - Wednesday

Monday, we got back to making love; but, Tuesday things were back to fighting as he ended up in a horrible mood after conversations with Jessie.

He threatens with every breath to not go to C_____. I guess if we make it to the airport by Saturday, okay. If not, oh well.

Sunday and Monday Jessie was conspicuously absent both in her phone calls and with Dion spending any time there. I suppose she is leveling some of her own silent treatment. But, Tuesday he had me drop him there after we had had a pleasant day shopping for clothes for our trip.

When she brought him home, he was different in that he had decided suddenly he didn't want to go to C_____ - and this after all the hell about "going back home."

Tonight the Jessie pattern continues as he: a) picks fights to justify leaving around 4:00; b) refers to her as his "employer" where he must pick up money.

Although I don't see any of the money, he does come home with new clothes, tools, and (admittedly) groceries. He has this thing about keeping me fed.

I want to say, "The reason I don't eat is because I am in such turmoil. How about keeping me emotionally fed."

We throw out most of the groceries he buys.

October 18, 19__ - Saturday

Dion was having such a guilty reaction to my having financed the trip to C_____ that Thursday I cancelled the trip. He said he has a new life and it is here in _____. He realizes that his life in C_____ is a thing of the past.

66

Thursday night he was so embarrassed at having cancelled the trip that he got back on the Schnapps and got crazy. I had to leave in order to get any rest Thursday night. I quietly slipped out and spent the night in the van. He was so devastated when I returned home Friday morning that he was a changed man.

We spent Friday together - he avoiding Jessie's 555 million phone calls; and, he promising to quit the heavy drinking. He threw out all the vodka, Schnapps, and Malt liquor bottles and began tapering off with a mixture of Clamato juice and beer. We made love like old times.

But, as always happens, we ran out of money, so it is back to Jessie's. She waves that money like a gigantic fishing lure; even drove her desperate self over here Friday when he wouldn't answer the phone; marched right into MY house (I was gone) and told Dion, "I have the money; let's go shopping."

Dion did a rare thing. He told her that I was gone and he couldn't just leave without telling me. He told her he was trying to devote the day to quit drinking, that he wasn't ready to just drop everything and leave. Told her to just leave the money and, "Rose and I will go shopping." This made her so mad that she stormed out, money in tow.

We went on to have a lovely Friday and most of today. Late this afternoon, after persistent annoying phone calls from her saying everything from: "Dion, I have the money," to "My car needs repair, can you look at it?" to "I want my cellular phone back!" (This cellular phone was a grand scheme of hers to be able to bypass my telephone and make private phone calls to Dion. Trouble was, he ignored the cellular phone, too.)

So: the current update is that Dion and I have just spent two glorious days together. We are very much in love and he proves very devoted to me. Granted, it pains my heart that he isn't in better health; but, I can only manage one day at a time and these past two days have been relatively alcohol-reduced and pleasant since Jessie's stress-evoking manipulations seem for the moment to have become rendered impotent.

October 19, 19__ - Sunday

Not only did Jessie buy Dion sacks and sacks of stuff, she also bought him a pint of Goldschlager Schnapps, a 6-pack of Jack Daniel Coolers, and a case of beer. Needless to say, Dion is out of his head again, back to abusive verbal slings: demanding that I sleep on the divan with him instead of the bed because he has bad dreams in bed.

He admitted last night that my observations about Jessie were right. He admitted he drinks more when he is around her. She is his trigger, he said. "Besides," he said, "she is ugly. Not a beauty like my Rose."

He is dying for an income. He realizes he must break free of Jessie; and, money is the only hold she has on him. At this point, I don't care if he spends every cent of his income on his projects. I can support myself; but Jessie is taking his life while she is trying to buy his company. The price of her money is too high.

I think part of the "ugliness" he speaks of regarding her relates to his realization that he is literally prostituting himself to her in exchange for alcohol. The loud, yet unspoken agreement between them seems to be that he will endure her romantic fixation in exchange for money.

But, these days my anger dissolves sooner and lingers less. My anger, (not only toward Dion but also toward Jessie) knows that ultimately Dion's life, as well as all life, is in the hands of God.

At times like these, I have nowhere else to turn except toward God. I have no choice but to say, "God, teach me the lesson in this. Restore Divine order."

At times like these, I reflect on the faith of Abraham, as he trusted God so much that he willingly offered his son as a living sacrifice.

At times like these, it becomes obvious that all of it: Dion and my deep, unrelenting bond of love, his anguished drinking and the debilitating effects of all of this madness must have a greater meaning than two people attempting to come together and live their life in the happily-ever-after-status-quo.

Maybe Dion's circumstance is a testimony to the truth: God gives and God takes away. Dion has defied death so many times. He defied death when they removed most of his pancreas ten years ago. He defied death when he slid down a snow-clad Rocky Mountain. He defied death, as he lay unconscious in the snow for who knows how long before he came to and began a brave crawl back up the mountain. He defied death our first trip to the beach when Jessie would not even allow us to be alone together long enough to plan our first private meeting together. He defied death just last month when they took one look at him at the hospital and literally sent him home to die, infection and all.

These days, I recognize this particular saga is about more than just what is good for Rose and who is the latest love of her life. This IS my life. My life has only just begun with Dion's arrival. On a spiritual level I know this.

I love Dion and deeply mourn his anguished disease.

October 23, 19__ - Thursday

Jessie continued to call and bitch and bitch about her car. "Why is it," she said on the answering machine, "when you're over here you'll work on the van; but, my car always gets put off until it never gets done."

So, Dion worked on her car Monday. Naturally, the Schnapps drinking began again that day. By Tuesday 2:00 a.m., he was talking out of his head; and, kept me up most of the night.

Wednesday, I went to work and welcomed being away from the house most of the day. Surprisingly, when I got home he was still home and was actually installing a new light fixture in the kitchen. Jessie called and I could tell from the conversation that she was trying to get him to come over. He put her off and actually spent the entire evening at home!

October 26, 19__ - Sunday

Friday, Dion brought me a bouquet of flowers and a beautiful card that read:

Since I met you, I've fallen in love with you at least a hundred times for a hundred different reasons.

Sometimes I fall in love with you when I watch you

Doing something you enjoy, something you're so involved in that you're unaware of my presence.

Sometimes I fall in love with you

When I listen to you

Talk to other people.

Whether you're being interesting and funny or warm and caring and genuinely concerned, you have a way of making people feel better with nothing more than your words.

Sometimes I fall in love with you just thinking about you, remembering all the memories we've made falling in love for the first time, staying in love during the rough times, finding more to love about each other each day. And whenever I think about the wonderful things that lie ahead of us,

I fall totally and completely in love with you all over again.

He seems to have had a realization or a change of heart. He admitted he needed therapy and purposely avoided Jessie's calls all day. He would say, "tell her I'll call back," or "tell her I'm in the bathroom" or "tell her I'm out." Finally he just said, "Unplug the phone."

He said he hated going over there. Said he needed to find a way to make his own money; so, we ran an ad in the newspaper soliciting handyman jobs.

Late in the afternoon we plugged the phone back in. Of course, it rang within about 5 minutes of being plugged in. Dion answered it very gruffly, determined to keep the conversation short, but it didn't turn out that way. He listened for a long time and turned white. When he finally got off the phone he was visibly agitated.

I said, "What the hell was that all about?"

He said, "She says she is broke and is going to have to sell her house unless we get this business started. She said she needed just 45 minutes of my time tonight because she had come up with some financial backers for our business."

My heart sank. Forty-five minutes, hell. Broke hell!

So, before we have a chance to think about dinner, off he goes to Jessie's house for "45 minutes of his time." I went to bed sick.

October 27, 19_ - Monday

Dion is recovering from the Sunday evening alcohol spree. He is very ill. He is too ill to pursue calls coming in off the ad he placed.

Very odd how he can make delicious love to me Sunday morning; then be on his deathbed Monday morning.

He is too ill to mess with Jessie's relentless phone calls. Although she did manage to get him on the line once, he refused to go over to her house to do whatever new odd job she had invented.

October 28, 19__ - Tuesday

Today Dion made an appointment for himself at the VA hospital's alcohol treatment program. He is feeling better healthwise. He unplugged the phone and this time we left it unplugged all night.

He cooked and we ate a good dinner. He "tapered down" from the latest spree with half a bottle of sherry, after having sweated out half a bottle of Kahula from Monday.

October 29, 19__ - Wednesday

Jessie came to complain so much about her car that Dion finally agreed to go over and finish work on it. This time, however, he insisted I come with him. Needless to say, one look at me and she wouldn't even SPEAK to Dion. But, at least he got the work done that she "needed."

Today was pretty much alcohol-free for him except for a beer at dinner. He says he could have sneaked drinks of the beer, but said he loves me too much to lie to me. I accepted that.

I decided to take this time to ask him, "Why does Jessie think you two have anything when you live with me?"

He said, "she knows she has nothing; that's what's wrong with her."

He is so troubled with insomnia. I bought him Aspercream to rub on his painful liver and bought him Valerian herbs for sleep.

October 30, 19__ - Thursday

The one beer at dinner Wednesday escalated to a 6-pack today and 3 little bottles of Goldschlarger.

After sending me on a midnight run for beer, I came back very upset by what he has reduced me to; and a fight escalated into terror. Although it becomes obvious that Dion is trying to break away from Jessie, I refuse to encourage or allow alcohol. He'll just have to go back to her for alcohol.

For me to buy the beer tonight could be construed as permission in his eyes; and I do NOT give my permission for him to kill himself.

October 31, 19__ - Friday

After working hard all day at some of his odd jobs, we went out for Halloween; but, not before a huge fiasco over how he had forced me to go out (no, I don't like going out -especially hate bars); how I don't like him.

Today's tally: 1 pint Schnapps, 1 quart Malt Liquor, 1/2 bottle Champagne, wine, Drambouie.

Since he has some of his own money now, the drinking is just as excessive. We fought over how I don't care about anyone; how he needs

70

to take care of his Mother. (Uh, yeah and I got some real estate in the swamplands I wanna sell ya).

NOVEMBER ONE

November 1, 19__ - Saturday

Dion made $200 today! He gave me $180 towards bills and kept $20. Although I find his contribution towards taking care of us encouraging, his obsession to drink persists. Today's consumption was 2 quarts beer and that horrible hallucinogen: Schnapps (one bottle of it).

We drove over to Jessie's together. He kept me waiting in the van for 2 hours while he tried to convince Jessie to buy some expensive tools he said he needed. Obviously, with me in the car, she turned him down so he came back to the car and said, "You're right. It is time to break the chains with Jessie. I need to buy these tools. Will you put it on your Sears card?"

Part of me knows he needs to buy tools to make money. The other scared part of me wonders: in his persistent stupor, does he really know what he is doing? My persistent compulsion is frugality. I said, "Dion, why don't you just wait until you make enough money to pay cash for what you need." He doesn't want to do it this way.

November 4, 19__ - Tuesday

Although Dion is working, I don't see the alcohol consumption slowing down much. I had hoped work would fill some part of his void. Today was another day of continued fighting over little stuff. In the middle of the day, however, we achieved a kind of calm when I managed to communicate something or other. But, for the most part, there is no consistency to his moods and I cannot count on any plan or good intention on his part.

Somehow, later in the day (I couldn't tell you the specifics that led up to this) I ended up asking him to move out. During these exasperated moments I come to believe that my relief over his absence will outweigh my missing him.

November 5, 19__ - Wednesday

Deep down I don't ever want Dion to leave. Sometimes I think my demands for him to leave are a manipulative tool on my part to force him to do things my way. I've become nuts and don't know what to do with my anger and frustration. Oddly enough though, were I to be honest with myself, I would admit that living without him is not an option.

He was supposed to have had 3 doctor visits today. One visit was to be with the GI Lab at 7:45 a.m.; one was to be with the psychiatrist; and, one was to be with the Priest. He got up this morning destroyed by yesterday's fight. He said since I won't marry him that he didn't intend to keep any of his appointments. He says he wants to die. So, here I sit out on a limb - all of my own doing.

Later in the day, Dion woke from a nap in a completely different mood. He woke on his own around 10:00 a.m. He was kind, quiet, and said he was going to work on the cars (at Jessie's) and then go see the psychiatrist this afternoon. However, I fear he has plans different than those voiced. I believe he wants to merely "smooth the water" so he can escape to Jessie's with the least conflict possible.

The day progressed fairly well until Dion began to press me to buy him a $150 memory cartridge for the digital camera he had gotten Jessie to buy. After I declined, he called Jessie and asked her TO COME OVER FOR DINNER! I told him I would leave the house if he did that. I refuse to serve dinner in my own home to a woman who refused to even let me walk into her house without threatening to call the police. He argues and argues with me on this point, but I refuse to budge.

By nightfall, we are in a screaming brawl with him threatening to smash the van windshield with a sledgehammer if I don't agree to rent a video - stupid stuff. I know our fight isn't really over a video. I just don't know what the fight is really about.

He took off in the van around midnight. It is 3:30 a.m. and he is still not back. I have to work early in the morning. He is probably passed out somewhere. As much as he drank today; and, as much as his stomach sticks out, he may be dead for all I know.

I am angrier with him than ever. All the Al Anon crap about not getting caught up in the alcoholic's insanity is going right out the window. How is it possible to maintain serenity when the "victim" has no safe place to sleep, has no safe place to protect her money so she will have enough to feed her four animals, has no regular mealtime, or bedtime? Dion's drinking has progressed to an all-time high and he blames me.

November 7, 19__ - Friday

After yesterday's hell, Dion was docile all day today. Determined to quit Schnapps, he really tried all day to be kind. I can see that he struggles to understand me. I see that he is afraid of my strong personality. In fact, he says he has never met a woman he couldn't conquer. He says I am stronger than he. He expresses feelings of inferiority with me; says one reason he hangs around Jessie is that she "makes him feel important."

Jessie called around 9:30 p.m. asking him to meet her somewhere so they could discuss getting a business license. It is nearly midnight and he is still out.

He says that after the business starts up, he wants to move on to music. That is fine with me. Physically, he pushes himself too hard in his work as a handyman. He won't stop to rest or to eat until the job is done; and, his health simply isn't that strong. As for this little "business" I keep hearing about, I am anxious for Jessie to take it and run with it. But, I fear two things: a) she may always be a nuisance; and b) this elusive, so-called "business" enterprise is but an excuse for Jessie to forge her way into Dion's future plans.

November 9, 19__ - Sunday

Back on the Schnapps yesterday after an all-night drinking spree

73

with Jessie buying as much alcohol as he could hold, Dion woke today very weak and sick. No more work has been done at her house - only drinking. He said today he must take to easy for a while; blames me for increased drinking; says 24 hours of me drives him to drink.

Jessie came by and picked him up at 4:00 p.m. to supposedly run errands, but I know he is down at the bar drinking because on Sundays no store will sell him liquor. He must be escorted to a restaurant with his "bottomless pocket" in tow in order to drink on Sundays. I have long since figured out why he finds

a reason to spend Sundays with Jessie.

November 15, 19__ - Saturday

After last Sunday's drinking spree, Dion nearly died AGAIN. Jessie told me she wished he would go ahead and die and I felt like screaming: I DON'T! I WANT HIM TO LIVE! I LOVE HIM! I WANT A LIFE WITH HIM!

His ascites returned, his blood pressure dropped, his blood platelets dropped; and, he has spent the entire week near death on the divan.

If his words can be believed, he sees what he has done to me and to himself and vows to devote every effort to change. The only thing I cannot get him to see or admit is how Jessie undermines our happiness and contributes to our demise.

November 16, 19__ - Sunday

With this, Dion's 7th sober day, things have returned to normal. Our lovemaking resumes. There is one difference this time: my attitude.

In doing my own soul-searching, I consider it probable that given my compulsive work habits, relentless verbal slings, and obsessive negativity (which include mammoth put-downs of Jessie), Dion seeks solace in the bottle.

For our battle over this horrible disease to become successful, I must commit to work on myself too. Among other things, I must watch what I say and keep pensive musings to myself.

I go back to work Tuesday; and, I pray Jessie doesn't manage to worm her way back in while I am gone. Dion hasn't seen her since the Sunday she so generously provided all the Drambouies he could down (the Sunday that nearly killed him); but, she calls EVERY DAY. Most of the time we don't answer the phone. Then, he calls when he feels like talking to her.

Yesterday, he yelled at her into the phone saying, "I don't feel like talking politics" (whatever that means). He slammed down the receiver and avoided her calls until she finally paged ON MY PAGER! Bitch.

November 20, 19__ - Thursday

After exactly 7 days of sobriety, Dion visited Jessie Monday (because I worked all day. I knew it would happen). When he came home, I thought I smelled alcohol. I did the worst thing I could have done. I mentioned it. All hell broke loose.

74

Having walked on eggshells this entire 7 days, I descended into exasperation and told him to move out. I said, "I look like a hag and I feel worse."

When I came home from work, he was lying on the sofa very angry and sullen. I could smell alcohol. He announced plans to have dinner alone. He left and stayed out until 2:00 a.m. or so.

November 21, 19__ - Friday

I worked all day again. I tried to be nice when I came home; however, he left and didn't come back until midnight. Naturally, he had been drinking. I decided to ignore it; not mention it. He confessed to it. We had a nice evening until I asked what I believed to be an honest question: I asked him "tell me how I cause you to drink." For some reason, this triggered an explosion from him wherein all hell broke loose again.

November 22, 19__ - Saturday

This morning Dion woke in a good mood. He announced plans to cook me breakfast. He sent me at 7:00 a.m. to the grocery store. Even though I suspected he just wanted to get me out of the house so he could call Jessie, I went anyway and had decided to keep to myself these suspicions.

When I returned home from the grocery store, Dion seemed in an agitated state. He said he had talked to the Priest and that he had scheduled a premarital counseling meeting for us. My heart sank because I knew that the Priest had advised against marriage until Dion quit drinking.

Dion picked up on my hesitation and misgivings and we got into one furious battle. He volunteered to leave; I felt lonely; he opened the first beer of the day. He said I didn't love him; would I get the sleeping bags so he could get away from me, etc., etc, etc.

I called a hypnotherapist for Dion and scheduled a Wednesday appointment.

November 24, 19__ - Monday

During the night Dion began to bleed profusely from the rectum, so we made a middle-of- the- night trip to the hospital.

Once home with the bleeding stopped, he went back out in the van to Jessie's no doubt, in that perpetual search for the drink. Meanwhile, I have gone way overboard in debt. I bought a car (he drives the van now), a computer (I needed one), a color printer (I needed one).

November 26, 19__ - Wednesday

Dion went to the hypnotherapist (surprise!); and, he emerged from the session in a better mood than I have seen him in a long time. But, this evening after I got home he was acting strange again. I suspect Jessie is behind this sudden chill.

After lying on the couch like a dying man, he got a phone call from Jessie; he immediately picked a fight. So, out the door he goes; gone, who knows where.

The fight was so stupid and petty I just left him sitting in the front room to fight with himself. He doesn't even make sense anymore. He is nowhere near quitting drinking even though he is obviously on his deathbed.

I believe he is grieving because I won't marry him; and, I believe Jessie is fueling the fire by putting words of doubt and despair into his psyche; but, I am completely helpless at this point in knowing how to deal with the two of them.

(Thanksgiving Day), November 27, 19_ - Thursday

For all the times I have said, "Thanksgiving is just another day," that flip remark threatens to haunt me as I ponder this, the first really challenging Thanksgiving Day I have ever spent. I truly didn't know what to expect or how to act around Dion. So, I decided that JUST FOR TODAY, I would act loving no matter WHAT CAME UP. I decided that nothing would upset me today.

Determined to have a happy day, I went to the couch where the crazed, sullen, sick and grouchy Dion lay. I kissed him, wished him a Happy Thanksgiving Day. This wasn't an act; I meant it. I love this man.

He continued to be cold, uncommunicative, hostile, distant, insulting, etc., etc., etc. Remarkably, I persevered. No doubt this is how I should have been acting all these months because as soon as I realized that Dion really does not posses the power to affect me, our day softened into love, kindness, joy.

The day ended on such a positive note that I could almost say, this was the happiest Thanksgiving Day I have ever spent.

Later in the day, Jessie called. She was very irritable. I asked how her Thanksgiving Day went. She barked, "fine; and you?"

"Wonderful," I said. "Today was a wonderful day."

She seemed startled and very shortly hung up the phone. I gather from that that she and Dion had plans to spend Thanksgiving Day together; however, that didn't materialize at all.

November 29, 19__ - Saturday

Jessie called this morning very upset that I was going to be involved in her and Dion's "little business."

I said, "Jessie, Dion asked me to help prepare the brochures. I bought a computer to do that and I intend to help him."

Then she revealed the REAL reason for her call. She said, "Well, I never know what's going on over there. First I hear that he is moving out ...."

"Wait a minute," I said. "Is that what this call is all about? Well, let me assure you Madam, if you are laboring under some misconception that Dion is moving out, you can forget it."

That was when I decided I would marry him.

Dion stayed with me all of today. Since the hypnosis, he has managed to kick the Schnapps and slowly, I notice an attitude change.

November 30, 19__ - Sunday

Although it is only 8:00 p.m., and most terror happens after dark, this has been a quiet, uneventful day EXCEPT that Jessie came over all decked out and wearing half a bottle of perfume. She banged on the door around 2:30 p.m. Said she needed to get back her battery charger. (She always repossesses the things she buys Dion when he stays away from her any length of time. She is very astute in her knowledge of how much power Dion's 'things' have over him. She seems to wield this power and play it as her last ace.)

Dion dutifully handed over the battery charger to her without an argument. She stormed out the door and in the time it took her to get home, she shortly faxed us a 10-page fax outlining payment expected for every receipt presented via fax of everything she had ever bought for Dion.

Exhausted, Dion slept most of the day. He ignored the fax. We unplugged the phone. I suspect he doesn't feel like fighting. His stomach sticks out horribly from the ascites.

The good news is that he had looked blankly at Jessie when she had charged in (she literally opened the door and WALKED IN without a knock). After much hand twitching, she left.

DECEMBER ONE

December 1, 19__ - Monday

God must be looking out for Dion and I because after not bringing in much of an income this month, we were hit in the parking lot by a large grocery store delivery truck. They ended up paying us $1,000. Damages to the van were negligible so we won't bother to fix the cracked rear tail light. We need the money for bills.

After Jessie left last night Dion became very sick and in pain. I thought we were going to have to make a trip to the hospital because he couldn't identify the pain. He was just in agony.

As if to aggravate the situation, Jessie called every thirty minutes (something she does when she has determined she WILL speak to Dion no matter what!).

We ignored the phone so she paged me. We ignored the pager. Then she called and left this message on the answering machine: "Dion, call me. This is very important!"

I erased the message from the machine. Nothing is more important than life and death; and, right now Dion is on the brink of death as I see it.

It is nearly 1:00 p.m. and he is still asleep. Only rest can cure him.

December 3, 19_ - Wednesday

Yesterday was peaceful; last night he was acting loving. Dion is not only very physically ill. He is also ashamed of his big belly. Despite this, matters between us have been delicious.

This morning a local film crew came to the house to film. In order to make money, I had volunteered our place to them to film a one-day project. Dion seemed ashamed of the way he looked and also a little mad at me for allowing his haven to be disturbed, so he took a pillow and went out to nap in the van. Before he left I asked him what was bothering him. He said the infamous "I have things on my mind."

Meanwhile, Jessie, ever mindful of new ways to barge her fat ass between us, called to offer to finish the business brochure AND pay for it. I told her to go ahead and do the brochure herself, since she not only hated everything I had attempted to do so far, but also she didn't want ME involved in any way in THEIR business. She had, to quote an infamous ex-President, "made that perfectly clear."

I'm sure Jessie broke her neck getting over here to pick up the brochure because she was here within 30 minutes of our telephone conversation. She went out to the van and tried to get Dion to come over to her house, but he declined. He MUST be dying.

Dion, still recovering, has not had a drink for several days now. However, he began to bleed again so we packed up and headed for the hospital.

Most of the morning consisted of sullen silence between us. Although it isn't unusual for him to become sullen and cold when he is sober, I had given him the cold shoulder after yesterday's enigmatic statement, "I have things on my mind." So, today I suspect he is returning the 'cold shoulder.' Oh, what silly games we play. Our love is right up there with the Greats, yet we play games and treat it so badly. Why?

While I waited for Dion at the hospital, I wrote a long letter to a friend back home pouring out my heart and my fears. It gives me a sense of renewed hope and fresh perspective when I find myself able to just talk things through. What, I ask myself, is the secret to loving someone and bridging the relationship difficulties long enough to be happy together? I am so weary of the drink problems.

December 5, 19_ - Friday

This morning Dion was angry because I got up early. I had left the bed, left him sleeping, and ran to do errands so I would be able to spend the rest of the day with him after he woke up. It seems only logical to me to accomplish tasks while he sleeps.

When I got back home and found him angry, I got into bed. But, he got up. Sometimes he seems to be just looking for reasons to hate me. At most, to avoid me. He probably thinks I am running off to be with someone else while he sleeps. That sounds like how his mind works sometimes.

He got up, got dressed and drove away in the van. Funny thing though, he called an hour later and said he felt lonely for me. I said, "Come home and lets have a good day."

He said, "you know what the fight is really about, don't you? Our real fight is about me being sick and you being healthy."

I said, "Dion, please come home. I love you. I would do anything for you. I just want us to kick this demon and have a life together." Then I said what I had been mulling over for several days. "Dion, I said. I love you so much I want to make an honest man out of you. I want to marry you."

Dion came straight home; but, later in the day around 6:00 p.m., the phone calls began. We ignored the phone. Then we unplugged the phone.

Well, you guessed it! Within the hour Jessie was banging at the door. Barging her way in, she asked if Dion was, "ready to go."

He, who was in the middle of preparing dinner, said, "No, it will be another 20 minutes."

I simmered in silence as I decided just this once to try to NOT REACT to this new knowledge that they had planned to go somewhere and work on that DAMN BROCHURE.

Dion asked me to transfer data from the computer onto the disc so Jessie could finish the brochure.

I said, "No, she hates the work I have done on the brochure so far.

Besides, she has offered to do it herself AND pay for it."

Although she left in a huff and Dion stayed and we had dinner and watched a movie in bed, the coolness remains.

December 6, 19__ - Saturday

Every morning the past few mornings Dion gets up and leaves to go to the van to have a drink. I pay no attention. Every morning about an hour later, he throws up. With his liver, he is never again to become able to drink, but he won't accept that.

This morning was another one of insults and the cold shoulder. Dion sometimes acts like a man who hates me.

December 8, 19__ - Monday

Saturday afternoon Dion finally broke the silence and talked to me. He says he is in constant physical pain. He says the ascites (which makes him look 6 months pregnant) makes him feel physically repulsive. I put my arms around him; he rested his head on my shoulder like a tired child; and I said, "Dion, to me you are beautiful. You are so handsome, really you are." And, I meant it.

Sunday was a quiet day of no strife. Strange as it may sound, I can feel God's hand in our finding one another. As I ponder about what day to get married, in my heart I feel this is the right thing to do. God has ordained us and sometimes I have to admit, I don't really know why. I just know He has.

Dion fills a void in me no human has ever touched. I found myself giggling today in the grocery store while we were shopping. There we were: he, swollen and dressed in his old shabby mechanics overcoat, his nails dirty from manual labor, wearing that half smile I love - the one where his eyes twinkle like the mischievous Scott he is. I giggled as I walked down each isle beside him. I giggled from joy just being with the man I love. To look at us I'm sure some would comment on our sloppy attire, but I never felt happier.

Dion was very weak and losing lots of fluid through the hole the hospital poked to drain the ascites. He has had to keep fresh towels over the opening, which leaks constantly. He is too sick to fight and lies on the divan fading in and out of sleep.

I worked until 5:00 p.m. today and returned to find him still on the divan. My heart goes out to him.

December 10, 19__ - Wednesday

Today was a repeat of yesterday. Dion continues to feel very weak from the loss of so much fluid.

When I returned from work at 6:00 p.m., he was gone. He said he went back to the doctor, but I think he probably went to Jessie's. However, he was home at 7:00 and slept the rest of the evening.

December 11, 19_ - Thursday

Our only outing today was to go grocery shopping. Then, Dion stayed in the van while I stopped at a couple of flea markets. But, after over an hour of shopping, Dion said he was too weak to endure any more, and asked to go home. Once home, he was barely able to eat and his fingers began to cramp so severely he couldn't hold anything.

December 12, 19__ - Friday

I worked this morning. Once home at 2:00 p.m., I was relieved to see that Dion looked better. But, a walk downstairs and the installation of my car tag left him too exhausted to do anything but lie on the divan. He continues to lose large amounts of yellowish fluid.

I used to be a very depressed individual. These days even though I have REAL problems, I am not depressed. Oddly enough, I feel fulfilled just having my love by my side.

December 13, 19__ - Saturday

Dion went back to the hospital where they stitched up the hole that had been leaking so much. I think they thought he would heal, but the hole had never closed up. They seemed concerned that he had lost so much fluid for such an extended number of days. Apparently, the loss of fluid had made him feel weak because he was losing pure protein. Also, his hands cramped because his electrolytes had become so out of balance.

We had a wonderful, yummy evening. I wish that he felt as healthy as I feel.

December 15, 19__ - Monday

I worked until 2:00 p.m.; then we went Christmas shopping. Back home we ignored the constantly ringing phone.

December 16, 19__ - Tuesday

I worked until 3:30 p.m. and got home to find Dion gone. No doubt he went to Jessie's because he came home at 5:00 p.m. saying she had money for the business project. Putting two and two together, I'm sure she called while I was at work, waved the 'money' flag, and here we are again off to the races.

I feel sure that all this "business project" amounts to is a drinking engagement. I say this because after these "business" meetings, I find small, shot-glass-size bottles of 15% alcohol hidden in coat pockets. I also found an empty pint-sized beer bottle in the van.

It has become easier lately for me to detach and keep in mind that all of this is really in God's hands. Also, it helps to write to my friend, which I continue to do.

December 19, 19__ - Friday

With me working more so Dion and I can have the money we need, Jessie has begun to move in again in my absence.

Wednesday I got home at 2:00 p.m. Her car was here, but the van was gone. So, wherever they have gone, they have gone together in the van.

Thursday when I got home, she had bought Dion cigarettes and left them in the van.

Today she called, thinking I was at work, no doubt. It will be a long day for me because I am babysitting tonight.

December 20, 19__ - Saturday

Just as I had feared, the same thing happened that always happens when I am away from home for any length of time: Dion hooked up with Jessie yesterday. Was that a surprise? After all, she HAD called bright and early in the morning, expecting me to be already out of the house.

So, yesterday, after he went out and she supplied him with his poison, he spent all of today near death, hemorrhaging badly from the rectum. He was so scared that he clung to me like a baby and he begged me to tell him that he wasn't going to die. He swore that since he met me he has been afraid to die because he loves me and wants to spend a life with me; saying he hadn't been fair to me regarding Jessie. He said that even though HE knew there was nothing there except spending money and expensive toys and meals (and alcohol), he wouldn't like it if I spent all my "down" time with another man. My heart said, "Thank you, Dion, for your honesty."

December 21, 19__ - Sunday

Three days until Christmas; and, if my life had a title right now, it would be, WAITING FOR DION TO DIE.

If it weren't for my few work hours spent doing temp work and running the occasional errand, I would never leave this museum-like house.

It is a sad sight to sit here at 9:00 a.m. on a spring-like Sunday morning watching blinking Christmas Tree lights and know that Dion, who is still asleep, will wake and be angry that I haven't stayed in bed with him until 1:00 p.m.

I look into the sunroom and whereas it once used to serve as a breakfast room, it now looks deserted and preserved like one of those birth homes of former Presidents. The 1890 Eastlake Victorian loveseat that I reluctantly kept from my antique store sits proudly, reupholstered and unappreciated except by lounging cats. The piano sits silent, as do Dion's guitars. There is a feeling of death in this house.

As for Rose, the nurse, the joke is on her. All this time she has foolishly kidded herself into thinking that as soon as the patient was cured, the fun would begin. Well, this question remains - Is the patient beyond recovery? Does the patient really want recovery?

Strangely enough, Dion has all but quit drinking. Yet, the damage is done. The one drink he has each day is ALL his body can handle; and, it keeps him sick all the next day. At least when he drank pints a day, the alcohol masked the illness and he seemed to have energy and personality.

December 22, 19__ - Monday

Today was a fairly uneventful day. I worked until 1:30 p.m. Once home, Dion, still in gown, dressed and went to the store for me because I was EXHAUTED. Jessie's calls started around 6:30 p.m. She had called once yesterday, but we let it ring. Nevertheless, Dion's trip to the grocery store found him smelling of alcohol. This makes me so angry that he will still, from his deathbed, continue to drink.

His one slip plus my weary exhaustion propelled us into a non-resolvable fight.

December 24, 19__ - Wednesday

I spent the day very depressed and attempted to call and reach out to some friends that I have, heretofore, ignored. As with what happens to untended friendships, everyone was too busy for me.

December 27, 19__ - Saturday

Despite my holiday depression, Dion and I ended up having a nice Christmas. We made real love and enjoyed the day all by ourselves, opening presents and taking pictures. Dion even set up the video camera and taped the entire morning of opening presents.

After all the presents were open, Dion found a reason for me to go to the back of the house and get him something. When I came back into the living room, I saw the video camera pointed straight at a beautiful gemstone, heart-shaped necklace hanging on the Christmas tree. This was a necklace we had looked at a long time ago on one of our shopping outings. How sweet of him to surprise me like this.

Of course, Jessie called all day Christmas Day. She left messages all day. She left messages all of yesterday, too; but Dion never called her back. Today, she called and left this irritating message, "since I haven't heard from you in a week." (No, bitch, we plan to get married.)

Admittedly, Dion is doing SO MUCH better. He hasn't really been drunk since Jessie nearly killed him that Sunday she so greedily enticed him to go to his favorite bar and bought his time with liquor.

Part of his newly found serenity is because of my newly found constancy. Even though I would bet he drinks one drink every other day (he has tapered down from every-day drinking), I try not to react and most of the time, I succeed.

Yesterday was somewhat of a family victory when my daughter invited Dion and I over for dinner. She cooked us a nice meal, but more importantly, they went out of their way to be nice to him.

December 28, 19__ - Sunday

We talked about setting a date to get married. I am marrying him despite the fact that he hasn't really enrolled himself into any kind of recovery program.

I had bad dreams and woke sad this morning. He woke grouchy. But, we persevered; we ignored Jessie's all-day-long intrusive phone calling. Ordinarily, she will stop at nothing to entice him away on Sundays. She couldn't possibly have any idea how close we have become.

December 30, 19__ - Tuesday

Last night we cuddled in bed and watched SELENA. We both were in a better mood today. Determined to marry tomorrow, I am still frightened to do so. But, to continue to merely "live together" with the one you really love is such a sham. Our devotion deserves marriage.

JANUARY ONE

January 1, 19_ - Thursday

We crossed the state line yesterday and got married. The marriage seemed to change both of us. I know I have done the right thing; and, Dion seems much happier. I watched him fight last night AND WIN the urge to go out and get alcohol. He got the cash and the alibi together (going to the video store). Then, at the last minute, he decided to stay home. He didn't need to explain anything to me; and, I didn't ask. I could tell by his almost shamed manner that he had been conducting a battle within himself the whole time. Both of us let the incident drop as silently and as effortlessly as a leaf falling on snow.

We ignored Jessie's calls that occurred every 30 minutes from the time we got home yesterday until 9:00 p.m. tonight, when she finally left a message for him to call. However, he never called her back.

January 2, 19_ - Friday

When I got home from work today, I got home just in time to see Jessie's car pull out. I was livid. Maybe part of this was my fault, however, because for some stupid reason, I told Dion that he didn't have to tell Jessie immediately that we had gotten married. I don't want him under pressure. I want peace of mind for him.

Now, I think telling him that was a mistake. Now, I think I should have called up the old bat myself and said, "We have gotten married; and, I would appreciate you leaving us alone. Don't call us. We'll call you." But, even I am not that heartless.

When I walked into the house I was already angry. Dion was tearful. He said Jessie had come by with money and said, "Lets go shopping."

Dion then told her (and for some reason, he teared up when he said this), "I can't just go and not tell Rose."

But, our tension escalated into a fight when I found empties of a large quart of beer and three little mixed drink bottles. Both of us tried to calm down.

We ordered a pizza; but, words flew back and forth: "You fall asleep during videos...........;"..... "Yeah, well you don't ever plan to tell Jessie we got married;"........."So! You didn't tell your kids.".........."I can't make you happy.............." on and on, both saying crap that has nothing really to do with our true argument.

I don't think he tries. He doesn't think I try. Are we incompatible? Maybe I'm nuts.

January 4, 19_ - Sunday

We spent yesterday with the kids; but, not before a huge silent morning where I literally walked out the front door, leaving him on the couch. Hours later, he paged me. I called him back and asked him to come over to the kids' house. SURPRISE! He came over.

More fights and hurt feelings as Dion left the house while I was working. He apparently went to the auto parts store with Jessie. Then he called me at 7:30 p.m. from a restaurant where he said he was having dinner and discussing "business." I slammed the phone down in his ear after saying, "I don't like my husband having dinner with another woman." Then I did a really dumb thing. I called my ex-boyfriend.

One thing I will say about having a conversation with my ex-boyfriend is that somehow I felt more calmly after talking to him. So, by the time Dion got home, I was calm. When Dion walked in the door he was sort of stooped over like a man who thinks he is going to be hit over the head with a rolling pin. When I smiled at him; and, then went up and put my arms around him, he looked at me like he thought I was crazy. But, he hugged me back.

January 8, 19 - Thursday

Dion is correct when he looks at me, goes into a depressed routine, and says, "you're not happy." All in all, we are pretty miserable together. Yesterday he was so despondent that all he did was ask me with that terrified look in his eye, "What's wrong?"

Stupidly, I attempted to explain, "You look miserable; you do nothing but sit on the couch and flick the TV remote; stare into space," etc., etc., etc.

Stupidly, I am drawn in each time to believe that when he asks, "what's wrong?" he really wants to know. Therefore, I am usually completely unprepared for his rote responses: 'I must be a terrible person.'....... 'I can't make you happy.'...... 'you always put us down.'...... When this happens, I am left believing he has drawn me out in order to fuel a fight.

We went to bed, two miserable souls barely speaking: he in the fetal position, me working on a powerful depression, all because we took one look at each other and said (almost in unison): "What's wrong?"

Of course, Jessie continues to call every day. That habit, in itself, is as maddening to me as the true water-dripping-Chinese-torture-routine.

January 9, 19_ - Friday

Today we had a long talk about how we hurt each other. Dion says he wants the same love and intimacy that I say I want. He says he is still reeling from hurtful things said last summer. He wants a rapid end to the troubles in our marriage.

He has started taking in car repairs to make money. He said, and rightly so, that as much as he loves me, he can't continue to sit on the couch and watch movies when there is money to be made.

He has also been pushing me lately to try to have some of my poems published.

He found us a poetry reading to go to tonight. It was fun and rather strange. My poetry might sound too tame, though, compared to the poetry read at this type of reading.

86

Dion came up with an idea to stage a three-day love fest for us. We began last night after the poetry reading.

This morning Dion took me completely by surprise by waking early (for him); and, we made love.

At 4:30 p.m. he started on his rounds to buy parts for the cars he is repairing. He got back at 7:00 p.m. and started dinner. He put on a Glen Miller Band tape to play and he told me to get dressed for dinner. I did. I put on my green lace evening dress; put my hair up in a black lace snood; and wore my rhinestone Lion earrings. He was shocked when he saw me come out of the bedroom.

We shared a beautifully prepared candlelight dinner to the sounds of Glen Miller and a ringing telephone. He turned up the music so it would drown out the telephone.

January 12, 19_ - Monday

I am shaking in my boots. Although Dion was up early working on cars, he told me that Jessie called while I was at work and said she had gotten together some "backers" who want to buy this idea he has for an invention. She had a meeting planned for tonight for him to meet with these "money people."

I begged, "Please Dion, don't go. You can make money by repairing cars. We don't need money. I'll work...." I said all kinds of things. But, as always, he tuned me out.

Around 7:00 p.m., he went to this big money-meeting-in-the-sky-turned-dinner-and-drinks-courtesy-of-you-know-who.

Having been gone 5 hours, he came home at 12:45 a.m., after having sworn he wouldn't be out until Midnight.

Obviously inebriated and with a fearful look on his face, clipboard in hand, he asked how I was. I said I didn't want to say, as it always led to strife. He assured me it was no better to keep it in and brood. I tried telling him for the trillionth time that Jessie was toxic for him, for me, and for our marriage. I tried reminding him how she has enabled him through bottomless liquor funds right into the hospital 4 times in the past 8 months. I told him I was sick of nursing him back from the brink of death only to have him go back over to her and gradually return to the gutter.

He denied Jessie had anything to do with anything concerning us. Then he let loose a barrage of insults, personal observations and sentences about me that did exactly as he desired. He made me angry. When anger enters logic, of course, exits.

Next thing I knew Dion said HE was leaving. It became obvious he intended to take the van. I told him he couldn't run off with MY car. He tried several ways to draw me into conversation that drew a conclusion telling him whether to go or whether to stay. I said, "do what you want to do."

Maybe he is fishing for reassurance, but I have told him my feelings many times. Maybe I did admit I won't tell my family we are married until he quits drinking; but, he hasn't told Jessie either.

I couldn't discern if he wants out of the marriage or if he was just testing me. Anyway, at 2:00 a.m., he called Jessie from the other room. I neither know nor care what they discussed.

January 13, 19_ - Tuesday

Jessie called bright and early at 8:00 a.m. this morning. We didn't answer. She called again at 8:30 a.m. I let it ring. I don't know what Dion, who was in the other room, did.

After our fight last night, he barricaded himself in the other room after I refused to continue the fight by saying, "YOU STARTED THE FIGHT. YOU FINISH IT. YOU DECIDE THE ENDING."

I am open either way. I am tired of endless fights. I am tired of clever manipulations. And, I am especially tired of planting seeds only to have them continually dug up. I take no stand whatsoever, since the outcome merely hinges on the mood of the moment or the beverage of choice.

After a morning filled with all of that turmoil, Dion left the house without a word and came back with a beautiful rose and a card. He was obviously distraught. He seemed to be trying very hard to understand me. The card was another one of those that expressed words I had often heard expressed from his own lips:

"You came into my life unexpectedly,
And everything took a turn for the better.
Your warm eyes, your laugh,
The sincere way you speak,
And the kindness you showed me
All became a part of my life.
As you unfolded yourself to me,
I discovered more and more beauty.
I have never seen so much gentleness
In one person.
Without even knowing it,
You were slowly making a place for yourself
In my heart.
It used to seem so hard at times
To feel close in a relationship.
But it is so easy to feel close to you.
I can't tell you how nice that feels.
I realize now that I had never known
What it meant to be loved until I was loved by you."

He signed it: Always, Je Temp (which French phrase he taught me the meaning of on our first date).

When Dion came in carrying the card and the rose, I felt sorry for him. His long blonde hair hung out beneath his felt, green, rimmed hat. He had drunk enough alcohol to adequately anesthetize him. In an intuitive flash, I saw him as a man trying to hang on, trying to cope, trying to understand his crazy, upside down world.

January 14, 19_ - Wednesday

Today I am feeling like a horrible person. The very act of being so self-centered that one can only see one's own agenda is a horror all its own.

Continuing to realize things from last night's unique breakthrough, I saw things today in Dion that I never noticed before:

1) He is nervous, delicate, and soft.

2) He is very intelligent and witty. Chatter that I used to tune out, I listened to tonight. His chatter is full of intelligent witticisms. No wonder he constantly complains that I don't listen to him. I don't!

3) He is very simple. Where did I perceive manipulation? Did I perceive them only in my own mind? He is so basic and simple that he resembles a good con.

4) He has a resigned, depressed, hopeless air that frightens me. He is easy to crush.

Tonight, Dion went to sleep saying he felt sad; that part of us had died; that I am out of his class. I felt horrible because I could see death of spirit.

He had just admitted to me that after that Monday that I had slammed the phone down in his ear that he hung around Jessie because she made him feel important.

May God help me. I can SEE my cruelty. I had assumed Dion was a man on my level attempting a relationship. In reality, Dion was a worshiper minus fight, minus con, whom merely adored me. And, in his adoration he was attempting to absorb all my abuse much like a battered puppy dog would have to do in order to get fed.

Part of realizing this is to acknowledge that I don't know if our relationship can ever be what I had dreamed. Had I assigned strengths to Dion that were a fantasy? He needs more attention, more understanding than ever I realized. I just might have to come down from my paranoid high horse to approach this simple man.

The Jessie thing is her fault. She hogs every minute with him she can because she is lonely and she gives not a flip what I think about it. He feels sorry for her; and he owes her $16,000 (according to her). I feel sure when he sees her he absorbs a huge amount of shame and guilt from her verbal badgering. He then looks to me, his wife, for support and all he gets are slaps in the face.

January 16, 19_ - Friday

I am determined to continue to treat Dion nicely. If he hasn't enough love to give me, it isn't his fault. He is kind and pitiful; and, I am determined to make his last days on earth happy.

Jessie has him again today. It is 5:00 p.m. and I am supposed to baby-sit tonight. I wanted Dion to come with me to the kids' house, but I see that isn't likely to happen.

January 17, 19__ - Saturday

Tonight at 4:00 p.m., Dion's usual parting time to go to Jessie's, he said to me, "I won't be long. Let's plan something fun tonight. What do you want to do?"

Knowing he was anxious to get one of the cars finished, I said, "Let's go to Sears; get the stuff you need for the car."

He said, "I want to go there when we can leave the van and stay until it gets a tune-up."

I said, "Let's go bowling."

He said, "There are other things to do besides bowling."

With tears behind my eyes I said, "Let's have dinner together."

He said, "Okay." Then he said we would shoot for 7:00 p.m.

He came home at 9:00 p.m. Fortunately, I managed not to lose my temper. We were able to salvage the evening by going to have a light meal and dance until midnight at the F_____ Club.

Later I found out he had to really tap dance to "escape" Jessie. I don't know why he told me this; maybe to show me that he was, indeed, trying. But, he said that he had to get downright rude and tell Jessie that he had to go and was spending the evening with "my wife."

I said, "Dion, you didn't tell her. I don't believe it."

Strangely, he didn't answer me.

January 19, 19_ - Monday

A weird occurrence happened that might have culled Jessie from our life once and for all. Around 5:30 p.m., Dion's Mother called to say she had received a phone call from an anonymous caller slamming "Dion's new wife" and hinting at revealing dirt on the new "in-laws." Dion's Mother is very dear to him and he got extremely upset to hear that she was upset. He stormed out of the house. I knew where he was going.

He returned from Jessie's to say that he had severed ties with her. That news is almost too good to be true. We'll see how she manages to worm her way back in. At any rate, he returned a buoyant man, one seemingly relieved of a weight; and, oddly enough, he hadn't had a drink.

January 20, 19__ - Tuesday

Huge fight ensued when at 9:00 a.m. Jessie called to see if "Dion was up yet." She said, "he said he was coming over here early to begin work." Then she said she didn't want to wait around all day.

Imagine my surprise! I thought she was out of the picture. I felt lied to; felt manipulated. This communication of frustration resulted in horrid hurt feelings on both parts. Dion went out; drank. He came back devastated. Said he was leaving the city; he will leave the business to Jessie and the cars to me. He said he has failed at everything he has attempted to do this year. He said he has nothing to believe in.

January 21, 19_ - Wednesday

90

Jessie drove over to the house and banged on our door. Dion told her to quit bothering us about that little business. He told her she was going to have to learn to communicate with ME! Consequently, she didn't call tonight.

January 22, 19_ - Thursday

I worked until 5:00 p.m. He was HOME when I got there. There had been no phone calls from Jessie. The loving mood begun from Wednesday's lovemaking had carried over to today. So, we went to a music store and bought a guitar cable; then went home and cooked a nice dinner together. We even went to bed early.

Dion said he wants to try and find an herbal or other substitute for alcohol.

January 23, 19_ - Friday

When I got home from work at 5:00 p.m., there was no Dion. After fixing up one of his cars for me to drive, he has now taken the van to drive, but there was no van at home. Once inside the house, I found he had left me a note telling me that he had taken the van to Sears for the work it needed. I felt sure Jessie was along for the ride, offering to pay. Dion isn't much better, allowing her to pay for repairs that were not her responsibility.

I decided that no matter what time he came home and no matter what shape he was in, I would NOT pick or respond to a fight. To tell the truth, I feel defeated; but, I have only myself to blame. I have failed at everything I have done, too.

January 25, 19_ - Sunday

Somehow a fight ensued after Dion and I went to a Super Bowl Party at his favorite bar. I didn't want to be there so what did I do? I got drunk. I am a terrible drunk. If I am combative as a normal human being, you should see me drunk.

All hell, which has been simmering since yesterday, broke loose today. Jessie called bright and early this morning telling Dion that her furnace went out; she didn't have any heat. So, the softhearted Dion, knowing her poor little self was freezing, took off early for her house.

January 27, 19_ - Tuesday

I said some horrible things to Dion last night. So, this morning he put his arms around me and said, "Let's forget last night happened."

I said I had no hope of things getting better; and I left for work without further discussion.

He called at midnight from Jessie's wondering whether or not to come home. She picked up the phone, disconnected us. I called back; she answered; hung up on me. I called back; the answering machine picked up. So, I don't care where he spends the night.

Before we got disconnected, I asked if he would go to marriage counseling with me. He said, "yes."

January 28, 19_ - Wednesday

Much heavy drinking as Dion continues to mourn. He had dinner with Jessie, I suppose.

January 29, 19_ - Thursday

Dion was home when I got home from work. Trying desperately to work things out, we had dinner together and went to bed early. But, he had a very bad evening spent in pain. I had to rub Aspercream all over his stomach and back. It seemed to relieve the pain. He begged me to stop triggering him to drink. I will try with all my might to reach an elevated level.

January 30, 19_ - Friday

Up early, we worked on cars together from 2:00 p.m. to 7:00 p.m. He had no alcohol today, but spent an entire day in severe pain. Jessie called all evening; we ignored, then unplugged the phone.

FEBRUARY TWO

February 3, 19_ - Tuesday

I must watch my attitude today. It is 2:00 p.m. and we are going out to work on a car together. I've been out all morning on what I consider to be wild goose chases. I have arrived at this point in the day feeling sorry for myself because I don't have a husband who "takes care of me."

Using some wisdom tips from the book <u>Soul Never Sleeps</u>, I managed to outlast my blue moods all through helping Dion work on the Toyota; plugged on through the beer he drank; persevered through all the errands run in the rain. We had dinner; watched two movies; made delicious love; ignored the ringing phone.

February 4, 19__ - Wednesday

The phone rang bright and early this morning at 10:00 a.m. Since the natural reaction to a ringing phone is to answer it, I did, forgetting for a moment how we are prisoners in our own home.

It was Jessie. She asked for Dion. I went in the bedroom; he said, "tell her I am asleep." I went back to tell her this. She didn't even bother to respond; she just hung up on me.

I went back into the bedroom, "Dion," I said, "we need to get an unlisted number." But, I could see from his disgusted reaction that this was not an option.

February 8, 19__ - Sunday

Thursday and Friday I worked all day long. Dion was home all day both days working on the cars. That Toyota truck is going to be the death of him. It seems non-repairable to me, but he won't give up on it.

I feel guilty for this because he didn't want to accept the job; and, I (who knew NOTHING about cars) talked him into it. Now, he won't admit defeat and call the customer to say: "I can't repair the vehicle."

When I got home today Dion was very sick. He said he was going to check into admitting himself to the VA sobriety program. Then he said that if he could abstain from alcohol for 6 months he would be eligible to get on a list for a liver transplant. Hope sprung in my heart to hear him talk like this. The physical work he has been doing on the cars seems to have given him courage and purpose.

Clearly, Dion enjoys me more each day.

February 14, 19__ - Saturday

VALENTINE'S DAY! What a lovely day it has been.

I worked all week last week. Monday, Dion worked on cars all day despite being sick. Tuesday and Wednesday he did more of the same. We hadn't heard from Jessie all week so Dion broke down and asked her to pick up some medicine from the VA because we both have been too busy to get over there. He had asked me first if it was okay with me. Stupidly, I agreed.

She has been calling like mad ever since. These days she doesn't even bother to acknowledge herself if I answer; she just hangs up in my ear. Her hatred of me, once smoothed over with a phony smile, is now blatant.

February 15, 19_ - Sunday

Today was a strange day. I had expected a continuation of yesterday when Dion cooked steak and lobster for dinner. Instead, he got mad at me on the way to Sunday brunch. He dropped me off at the restaurant while he was gone almost 45 minutes getting batteries for the camera. We ended up not eating; went back home. Jessie had called at 3:00 p.m.; called and hung up while he was in the bathroom at 4:00 p.m. At 5:00 p.m., he is out the door. I am beginning to hate Sundays.

February 16, 19_ - Monday

Today I was made privy to Dion's strange behavior yesterday. He had seen a sizeable check Mother sent to me; and, this made him feel betrayed. Up to now, he has felt proud of himself for working to bring in money "to support his wife." But, according to him, seeing this large check from Mother made him feel that he wasn't providing for me adequately.

This latest sensitivity set off another drinking spree, which set off serious illness, which translated into him going to Jessie's and staying until midnight.

I am beyond rage. This is sheer insanity. Maybe he died. Who knows.

February 17, 19__ - Tuesday

Dion came home around midnight VERY SICK. In the night, he nearly died from an apparent pancreatic attack. He only has left a pancreas the size of a quarter. Nine years ago, after some sort of new, experimental pancreatic surgery, he was given only two weeks to live; it is a miracle that he has lived nine years.

It is now 12:15 p.m. and he is still sleeping. As I tiptoe around the house, it occurs to me that he may be lying in there dead. I resist the urge to go out and run errands because when I leave he becomes very suspicious and inquisitive with strong hints to my abandonment. Amazing what double standards addicts have.

I seriously doubt if Dion will live to see his 47th birthday coming up in three days. This has clearly been a year of suspension on my part. I have lost all contact with any friends I once had. To all that I have just said, Dion would likely comment, "Having quite a pity party, aren't we?"

February 18, 19_ - Wednesday

We passed a very difficult, if pleasant day. He was very ill. No wonder he becomes disillusioned when he quits drinking. His symptoms (the ascites and pancreatic ache) get worse! This seems to be because when not drinking, he eats a lot! His belly protrudes even more because his liver cannot handle the food.

Even so, after having the phones turned off all day, his first day of sobriety, Miss Selfish Bitch Enabler Blackmailer FAXED him a note: "Dion. I am having car trouble. Please call."

Car trouble my ass!

February 19, 19_ - Thursday

Jessie called at 1:00 p.m. I answered; handed phone to Dion. She asked him to do a tune-up on her car. He asked my permission. I said, "go ahead," knowing his two-day sobriety would immediately be compromised; yet also knowing if I denied him, his sobriety might still be compromised AND he would be mad at me.

It is heartbreaking to watch someone in pain. It is heartbreaking to wait for the next drink like one is waiting for a land mine to explode.

I realize that my morbidity over this has reached hideous proportions. The obvious scapegoat for me is Jessie. Even though I recognize the big problem is Dion's refusal to sever ties with her. I can (and do) get furious at her for continuing to wedge herself between us; but, I know (and she knows) that Dion isn't strong enough to stop her.

When I react, he drinks. This appears to be truly a hopeless situation. He promised me sobriety for his birthday, which is tomorrow.

Jessie knows he is trying to absent himself; yet, she won't leave him alone. After a few days go by without him calling her, she dreams up any excuse she can find to call him. Today his excuse was a tune-up. Yesterday, it was car trouble. The month before it was mysterious "backers with a lot of money," and on and on.

I don't feel there is any ground to be gained for me to continue to force the obvious issue. As evidenced by Jessie's past actions, if Dion succeeded in making a complete break with her (for the millionth time) she would just continue to make our lives miserable (this time she might even repossess the tools he uses to repair cars).

It is obvious that if I really care about my beloved's health, the compromise is up to me. Keeping my rage at bay is my most difficult challenge.

February 22, 19_ - Sunday

I spent most of yesterday babysitting my grandson while I waited for Dion to do Jessie's "tune-up." He arrived home at 10:00 p.m. falling down drunk. It was all I could do to be civil to him.

Today, sensing my despairing resignation, he "talked a good game." He said he had let me down constantly. He said that he was actually looking forward to kicking alcohol. But, when he left at 2:00 p.m., I knowing he probably wouldn't be back until midnight and probably drunk, at that, went to have dinner with the kids. I called the house at 9:00 p.m. There was no answer.

February 23, 19_ - Monday

This is no longer a matter of anger; but it is one of acceptance. Even the dog is suffering after eight months of having Dion live with us. I thought the dog had sharply reduced his barking and tail wagging. Then I noticed one morning when I let him out to pee that he didn't feel confident enough to run up the stairs. He sat at the base of the stairs as if waiting for me to pick him up. Then, last evening when I took him with me to the kids', my daughter remarked, "B_____ (the dog) surely has aged."

I have up to now been in deep denial about Dion. He has great expectations for himself regarding the VA Sobriety Program, which begins tomorrow. He has appointments with the Social Worker for interviews. He says he is going to ask to be admitted for five days. But, I have no hope for him. I believe him to be one of the 88% of alcoholics never cured.

Love is not enough to wage every war. Amidst troubled tears this morning, Dion said, "I love you so much it is devastating. Yet, I don't know how to take care of you. I haven't been able to give the special kind of care required for someone as special as you. Some things are very delicate. There is only one Mona Lisa."

All this pretty talk I have heard before in one way or another. Yet, after his nap, he got up as sullen and angry as ever.

I doubt he will ever change enough to be able to make me happy despite our desperate love for one another.

February 24, 19_ - Tuesday

Dion went to the VA to have the water drained from his belly; and, begun his first day of sobriety.

February 25, 19_ - Wednesday

Dion spent most of today recovering. Jessie called to say her furnace needed repair. He declined.

February 26, 19_ - Thursday

Dion's third day of sobriety found him well enough to resume his work on cars. Also, he went to bed early.

February 27, 19__ - Friday

God allowed a strange monkey wrench to be thrown into our lives today. I had accepted a job to be an extra in a grocery store commercial because it paid $150. We had to start the job at 10:00 p.m. because the store needed to be free of customers. Never in my life did I DREAM the job would run ALL NIGHT. But, it did.

When I got home this morning at 7:00 a.m., I could tell by Dion's ravaged face that he didn't believe I had worked all night. I don't blame him; I wouldn't have believed it either.

He has been doing so well the past few days with his sobriety efforts that I immediately regretted having taken the job. There was no way I could convince him that I was telling the truth. He refused to believe anything except that I had "been with another man." What is worse, he said, "I don't blame you. I have treated you terribly. You deserve more than this."

I could have died. Nothing I could say or do would ease his mind. I even showed him my signed contract that showed quitting time to be 6:30 a.m., but he still refused to believe me.

February 28, 19_ - Saturday

I stayed in bed until Noon, like Dion likes for me to, but he still got up this morning cold and non-responsive to me. He tried to deny his punitive silence; yet, walked out the door with little more than a cool brush of hands saying he had "errands." I'm sure his first errand is to fix Jessie's furnace.

Dion came home at 7:30 p.m., drunk. But, he tried his best to make peace.

MARCH TWO

March 1, 19_ - Sunday

Both Dion and I were anxious to get along so the air between remained rather polite but stiff. I puttered around getting things ready for a garage sale the end of this month. He left at 4:30 p.m. to get money for fixing Jessie's furnace.

Since the kids were waiting for us to come over and have a nice Sunday dinner, I threw a mini-fit saying, "don't leave now. You won't be back in time to go over to the kids'!"

But, he did come back in time. He even took his guitar and gave guitar lessons to one of the visiting relatives.

I am acting wrongly; and, I can feel it. Dion attempts to be kind; but, something has happened to my trust. It is difficult for me to continue to show adoration. This bothered him; and, he fretted all night in his sleep. Almost made me feel guilty. I have been there for him up to now. What has happened to me?

March 2, 19_ - Monday

Poor Dion. He got up this morning to stony silence. He left. Called from Jessie's at 2:00 p.m. We talked.

He said he wants to try again. I thought: *I have been trying all along. Where have you been?*

Oddly enough, I find dim hope abides in my heart. He continues to improve while I deteriorate. He begs me to acknowledge his changes. He says, "people comment on how much I have changed."

But all that rings in my head are the words to <u>Send In The Clowns</u> about how now that "......you here at last on the ground; I, in mid-air......"

Daily, I become the Portrait of Dorian Gray. Dion brings out the worst in me, I fear. He rouses all of the insecurities that I possess.

We talked out our fight; yet, my feelings remain unchanged. He left the house at 9:30 p.m. to meet Jessie at the "Waffle House" so she could "give him $50 of the $200 she owes him for his work on her furnace."

Isn't it strange that she cannot give him the money here at the house; yet, she can certainly barge into our home for any other means when she can't manage to intrude by telephone? Even as I say all this, I know my heart is not right or I would find forgiveness, understanding or some kind of resolve for Jessie's influence in our lives.

He got back home at 11:30 p.m. acting, yet not smelling, like he had had a drink. He said Jessie had opened a $2,500 line of credit for him to begin work on his invention. I shook my head and said nothing.

Since he has money, Dion went out the first thing this morning to get soup (yeah, right). He came back 30 minutes later nauseous. After he recovered, he left and stayed gone until 11:00 p.m. Returned drunk.

Went out to his favorite bar to get food. Returned drunker.

March 4, 19_ - Wednesday

Dion had worked himself into a volatile and extremely emotional state of mind just contemplating working with Jessie on his invention. He, in his drunken stupor, maintained that only I could harm us; only I could prevent this invention from being successful. Then, he began a tirade that forced ruin upon the day. He demanded that I tell everyone that we were married. I found myself telling him I wanted a divorce (something that couldn't be further from the truth. He just makes me so angry!).

The fight escalated until I told him I hoped he would die. That brought tears to his eyes and to mine. The fight went right out of him; and, the breath went right out of me.

I had never been this angry before with the exception of the one time back in his apartment when I was so enraged that I threw every empty Schnapps bottle I could find right at him. Watching him dodge the bottles was the only thing that snapped me back to my senses.

Jessie arrived at the house at 1:30 p.m. with $300. He made her wait outside while he tried to get me to say I loved him. I was so stubborn that I wouldn't say it. I kept running images through my mind of all the nights he left me here alone while he spent endless hours of our precious time drinking.

I must find a way to forgive him. Why have I suddenly frozen up? Even as I ask this, I know the answer. I am afraid of continuing to hurt. I hurt so much that I want to cry out, "please let this cup pass."

Dion stayed at Jessie's until dark (what else is new). He called me to say that Jessie has offered to "store his stuff at her house," (I can see her drooling already) while he makes plans to move to the beach.

I am hearing and feeling all this stuff like a mind gone blind. A large part of me hopes he does move to the beach. I am numb.

March 5, 19_ - Thursday

Dion came home last night at 4:00 a.m.(his usual bedtime) falling down drunk. I left him sleeping this morning and went to work.

March 7, 19_ - Friday

Although most of our fights have been about Jessie, today Dion and I fought off and on like queasy children over some unnamed nothing. Our fights were small and petty; and, we didn't even know why we were fighting. It almost seems that we have lost track of all the problems that need to be resolved; and, we seem to be fighting our way back through the mist trying to find them.

When I left the house to go to a birthday party for the kids, Jessie had called to see if the "coast was clear" to come over. So, it didn't surprise me when I got home to find that the two of them had shared a cozy dinner. She was sitting (IN MY HOUSE) back in the office, her shoes off; and, I heard him remark to her, "I guess now that she is here, you are going to leave."

I had spent the entire evening in prayer because I felt trapped and found myself planning ways to run away from my problems. God seemed to say to me: "Dion is in pain about the marriage being kept secret." I had told the kids we were married; and, decided to do the same to Miss Jessie.

So, I marched into the back room where Dion was working on blueprints and Miss Bitch sat unwelcome in my house. I looked at her and I said, "Did Dion tell you we got married?"

She maintained that phony smile through clenched teeth and asked, "When did you get married?"

"December," I said. Then, I left them alone while I cleaned up the kitchen mess.

I heard yelling coming from the room. I heard her demanding "all her stuff back."

When I heard that blackmail talk again, I marched back in the room and addressed her ugly, screwed up face, "Why are you demanding all your stuff back? What has changed?"

She jumped up and said, "I can't STAND you. I think you're evil. You're mentally ill. You're self-centered; and, you HURT people."

I felt that psychic punch hit right in the pit of my stomach. I said, "Come, come, you aren't allowing your Christian heart to judge me are you?"

She spewed her continuing tirade, "everyone I know thinks you're evil."

I said, "you must have some evil in yourself to be able to see evil in me."

She huffed past me. I said, "Besides, I have never heard you say a kind word about anyone."

The minute she got home, she faxed over a receipt for every tool, and every piece of equipment, every meal, and every item she had ever bought for Dion.

After having vented my rage upon the proper person (Jessie), my feelings toward Dion softened. I didn't know, nor did I ask, how he felt at the moment.

One thing I do know for certain: now that Jessie knows Dion is married, if she still continues to call him to fix her car, fix her furnace, fix this, fix that, she will not be abiding by her Christian teachings, will she? Besides, I'll just bet she wouldn't allow another woman to call her husband.

As far as I am concerned, Christians like Jessie give Christianity a bad name. People like her alienate non-believers.

Dion expressed relief after she left; and, admitted that to continue to have to receive her affections for money made him feel like a gigolo. We both seemed to find release from our previous nebulous fighting; and, that was enough for the moment. We could both breathe again; and, in silence we left it at that.

March 7, 19_ - Saturday

This turned out to be another Jessie-fiasco-day. Dion and I played music all day, ignoring his previous "work assignments" on the "invention." He drank steadily all day. But, at 7:00 p.m. Jessie called and he met her at his favorite bar where they stayed until 2:00 a.m.

March 8, 19_ - Sunday

Holding my possessions over my head as she had heretofore held Dion's "purchases" over his head, Jessie attempted to hold my van seats hostage. Seems Dion had stored the seats at her house while he was cleaning the carpet in the van; and, hadn't put them back in yet. She made some lame comment that if I attempted to come over and get the van seats, she would call the police. (I am only assuming that it would be allowable for only DION to come over and RESCUE the van sets.)

But, I went over to her house while she was at church and got them. Idiot that she is, she had left them out on the carport where Dion had probably set them, namely because I don't imagine she could move them since they weighed a ton. Nor does she possess the intelligence to mastermind a really good

Heist by hiding them away somewhere. Dion is right; she really isn't very smart.

Don't ask me how I hoisted those 100-pound seats into the back of the van, but I did. Anger is a great motivator; and, I guess where there is a will, there is a way.

When I got home, Dion was awake and sullen that I had left his sleeping side early in the morning. He said to me, "I miss you when you are gone. Even in my sleep, I miss you."

Near midnight Dion began to bleed from the esophagus so we went in the middle of the night to the VA hospital.

I was feeling so upset and defeated that while I waited, I wrote a five-page letter to him explaining why I had to leave.

When we arrived back home at 5:00 a.m., while he was in the bathroom, I left the letter and fled to the kids' house.

March 9, 19_ - Monday

My daughter brought me back home at 6:00 p.m., where I gathered enough clothes to last a week; then, went back to her house.

I left behind the letter to Dion, which included instructions to clear out. Then I left a nasty letter in Jessie's mailbox explaining to her how she had interfered so selfishly in our lives that she was destroying Dion. I told her one of us had to let Dion go since he hadn't the courage to set things right himself. I believe I told the truth when I told her that to continue to fight over Dion like he was a rag doll was tearing him in half. She may be, but I am not willing to stand by and let that happen.

March 10, 19_ - Tuesday

I went back home to feed the cats. I saw the truck Dion has been working on had been slapped with a bright orange tow ticket. I called Dion at Jessie's to tell him that someone must have complained; and, now the vehicle was in danger of being toed away.

He didn't want to talk to me in front of her. He said, "let me call you from the fax phone in the other room," (a separate line where she couldn't listen). When he called back, I didn't answer. I am sick of all this manner of deceit. If he cannot talk to me in front of her, he cannot talk to me.

March 11, 19_ - Wednesday

From the kids' house, I called home and Dion answered. He said he was staying there until I came home. He was devastated. Said he had broken all ties with Jessie. He said every syllable of my letter to Jessie was true. I went back home only to find the phone ringing off the hook. For the nth time, we unplugged the phone.

Dion said he would go with me tomorrow to talk to the Priest about our problems.

March 14, 19_ - Saturday

Friday, we went together to talk to the Priest. He said Jessie must be completely severed from our union. Dion, acting like he had never before been aware of my pain in this matter, apologized to me.

Today we spent a quiet day together. Dion is trying very hard to get along with me. He said he told Jessie not to call. Yet, around 5:00 p.m., she called. He was short with her on the phone. After a very brief conversation with her, he hung up the phone and told me that he must be more firm with her.

March 15, 19_ - Sunday

We went to church together; then played tennis. We discovered all the tools had been taken from the car he was working on. My first suspicion was that Jessie took them. As I told the Priest, she is especially creative in finding ways to interfere in our lives. This latest 'theft' seemed to be one of them; as, Dion is now completely helpless to continue to work on cars and earn a little income.

I am so scared. I fear that she is going to find a way to break Dion's 5-day sobriety with all the vicious turmoil she levels against our marriage.

March 16, 19_ - Monday

Dion called Jessie to demand that she return the tools. He apparently struck a note of finality with her because she called back demanding back all the musical equipment. Oddly enough, Dion took things back with me in the car; and, he didn't linger to talk.

March 17, 19_ - Tuesday

Quiet, uneventful sober day. Dion and I went to Sears where I let him buy and charge every single tool he needed to continue to work on the cars.

When we got back home Jessie had faxed a note saying, "I didn't mean to cause trouble."

I could die. I could literally lie down and die. I want to run out into the streets and bang on doors and beg people, strangers, to PLEASE HELP ME! A NEW KIND OF ALIEN IS ALIVE AND WELL AND RUINING TWO LIVES!

March 18, 19_ - Wednesday

Today was a lovely day even if all we accomplished was to hang wallpaper.

This is Dion's 8th day of sobriety. He is happier, more talkative than he used to be when sober; so, I assume he is at peace. I wish I could say the same for myself. I continue to walk on eggshells; fearful; unable to forget horrible feelings of the past; fearing his drinking; fearing Jessie.

Today I went to work. It will be the first time in 9 days I have been out of Dion's sight. I fear.

March 24, 19__ - Tuesday

It takes incredible honesty to admit this; but: with Jessie out of the picture to take the financial heat off, I feel myself approaching a mental breakdown. Financially, we can no longer pay our bills so a new form of tension has set in. Also, I have to admit another painful realization: I fear closeness.

Before we married, I had been divorced so long that I became spoiled. I realized this one day when Dion said, "I don't think we can afford for you to go home to see your Mother right now."

I took offense. I took offense KNOWING that he was right. My first reaction was to ask him how he felt he could tell me what to do? Then I realized that he was right. We are married now. This should be a joint effort.

March 27, 19__ - Friday

After watching me sort of "crack up" Wednesday and Thursday, Dion softened his oppression long enough to allow me to breathe.

It is amazing how many things can happen in only two days. They cancelled our Texaco card for lack of payment, so Dion has been forced to come up with his own money for gas and cigarettes.

Also, backed up against the wall regarding car repairs (which drink, illness, fights and recovery extended four months) the local homeowners voted to tow ALL the vehicles.

Enter Jessie. She had the vehicles towed to her house AND PAID FOR THE TOWING. So, now the plan is that Dion will have to work on cars at her house.

I cannot honestly say Jessie did us in this time. Fate did us in. The very eternities seem to be fighting against this marriage.

March 28, 19_ - Saturday

Although he won't admit it, I know Dion went to Jessie for money yesterday and the day before.

He came home late, drunker than ever, saying how good it was to be with me (some odd thing he always says after spending time in her company). And, later, angry that his Lionel Richie tape didn't adequately serve to express his "deep love" and make me forget his neglect of me, our life together, our responsibilities, and our finances, he lashed out with loud verbal abuses calling me those names parroted from Jessie's mouth: evil, self-centered, hurtful.

My prayer is that God will end this madness soon.

March 29, 19_ - Sunday

When I came home from work, Dion was gone. I saw Jessie's car at his favorite bar. By this, I gathered that they spent the day together in the bar.

I left a note telling him once again to please move out. Then, I left and spent the night with the kids again.

I have to admit one thing: the kids will probably never again accept Dion as they once did. I also have to admit that their intolerance of him is my fault. I should be woman enough to stay in my own home and keep my own fires quieted. But, I am so emotional lately that I am almost at the breaking point. I need the comfort of family around me.

March 30, 19_ - Monday

When I came home later this evening, Dion was not there. I gathered more clothes for another night's stay at the kid's house.

I had called him from work this morning. We argued. He denied having been with Jessie Sunday. He said he was working on cars all day. He said he didn't know why Jessie's car was at the bar (this is probably one of his most outrageous lies yet).

March 31, 19_ - Tuesday

Dion called me today very upset. He said he had talked to the Priest; and, the Priest had advised that he do as I say and leave. He asked if I would just give him 30 minutes of my time first. I agreed to do so.

We talked for 30 minutes. He expressed all the things he has always expressed: dismay at losing me; helplessness at knowing how to solve our problems; assurance that he loved me, etc., etc., etc.

I feel the same way. I love him as always before. The difference is that I can no longer find a way to change things. I no longer know how to work on our difficulties. We have tried marriage counseling (I am the only one continuing to go). We met with the Priest (whose words of advice served us for maybe a week).

APRIL TWO

April 1, 19_ - Wednesday

Home from working on cars at Jessie's, Dion carried a long-faced, martyred expression. He said he would call and check with me each day to see if it was okay to come home.

It is in times like these that I see a glimpse of a Dion who truly does not understand that my reaction to him is in response to his treatment of me. This type of merry-go-round set in motion by the disease is precisely the reason why I should be going to Al-Anon. Why won't I attend the meetings regularly? I try to apply their principles, but it isn't the same as gaining reinforcement from a loving group. Yet, I haven't committed myself to the group long enough to FEEL any loving support. What vicious cycles we perpetuate.

After having spent some restful time away from Dion, I find Dion's morbidity excessive. I feel sorry for him. He acts like a troubled child who is trying to do the right thing. Has his drinking deteriorated his mind to the extent that he does not see his contribution to our pain?

April 2, 19__ - Thursday

Dion and I had gone to see the marriage counselor together. Afterwards, he seemed to gain a better appreciation of me; and, he was prompted to say that he felt he knew me better. He said, "I can see why you are scared of me."

Funny, I hadn't realized that I WAS scared of him, but I am. We both seemed more relaxed after our session.

April 3, 19_ - Friday

Today was a day completely sober for Dion. We had fun; and, cooked out on the grill.

April 7, 19 - Tuesday

Saturday became strained. On Sunday, Dion found a drink, but we managed to pass the evening in a civil, if strained, manner.

Monday, Dion went to Jessie's and drank a little bit of something. Then, today, he went over there and has stayed all day working on cars. Oddly enough, Dion has called me every hour or so. Is he checking up on me? I feel chained to the house. I don't want to leave and give him the impression that I am not trying to work on this marriage.

At 4:00 p.m., he called to say he was headed home. I waited an hour, then began to get angry. I figured Dion was NOT really coming home, but was just calling every hour or so to be sure I was home. So, I called a friend and made plans to go to a movie.

I left Dion a note telling him I had gone to a movie. Let him see how it feels to be 'betrayed.'

But, the joke was on me because after I returned back home from the movie, Dion was STILL NOT HOME!

Shortly after I arrived home from the movie, the phone rang. I suppose Dion had been calling home all evening. He asked, "is it safe to come home?"

My anger dissolved, I said, "It is always safe to come home. I miss you. I love you."

He came home a couple hours later (yes, by now it had become VERY late at night; but, for the night owl, Dion, late nights are nothing). Surprisingly, he was not drunk.

He held me. We made love. We giggled. We laughed. It stormed outside. The electricity went off at 1:00 am. We didn't go to sleep until around five.

April 9, 19_ - Thursday

The witch is after Dion's butt again. She called at 9:00 a.m. asking, "Is Dion up yet?"

Wimp that I am, I said, "No, he isn't," instead of saying: "what business is it of yours?"

But, I find it almost humorous now how her little game explodes in her face sometimes. Every time Dion gets into her for a few bucks (and she spent plenty on him last night) she thinks she owns him, when, in fact, all she really owns is more debt.

I have begged, pleaded, bitched, screamed, cried, prayed, manipulated, threatened, but Dion won't stay away from her, her bribes, and her money.

Tonight, after spending all day over at Jessie's (once she got him out of bed by her constant calling), Dion came home at 10:30 p.m. very drunk. Just as I had sat down to eat chili, he asked if he could take me out to eat. Since I figured his invitation would include alcohol, I declined.

He ended up going to bed without food or medicine. I should have stopped catering to him a long time ago.

April 10, 19_ - Friday

Dion got up in a bad mood, wanting to fight. I refused. For myself, I must wake up and quit being a martyr. I must resist the urge to use Dion's shortcomings to make myself look good. I must stop viewing myself as a victim except to my own self-perpetuating destruction.

Dion has helped me more than anyone to see that self-examination should be just that. It should not include other people's faults and how it bounces off other people's behavior. Such honest examination is our only hope to stop this destructive merry-go-round of alcoholism.

I will TRY to record my feelings; and, when it comes to Dion's actions, I will try to find what hidden flaw of mine I attempt to "explain away" by focusing on HIS actions.

Dion got so sick that Jessie actually brought him home (although, I later found out that he had to DEMAND that she bring him home). He said that every moment with her is agony.

106

In getting to the bottom of this latest "falling out" with her, it seems that she became resentful that Dion gave ME the money from the insurance company for the stolen tools. She said it was SHE who bought the tools in the first place. Technically, she is right. Well, guess what. Screw her.

April 11, 19_ - Saturday

Today I dropped Dion off at Jessie's to do, to quote him, "one last day of work; and, then I will never go around her again."

He claims that in their heated discussion yesterday he called her a sanctimonious hypocrite when she pitched a fit about me getting the insurance money. His exact words were (according to his version) "Screw you. Rose needs the money. She works as hard as you do."

April 12, 19_ - Sunday

Today, Dion and I had planned to go together to the kids' house for an Easter Egg Hunt. I had dyed eggs, made baskets, and bought presents. He decided after coming in late last night that he wanted to go to church to the 6:00 p.m. Mass because he wanted to "work" (or so he said) and "get paid for the engine." He promised to come to the kids' after he got the engine fixed.

I drove over to the kids' house, feeling very alone. There is just something about holidays that magnifies aloneness. Somehow, around 4:00 p.m., I KNEW Dion had no intention of coming over. I knew he had no intention of ever being a family, of ever doing the right thing, of even keeping the church date tonight. I was there in the kids' house "alone again, naturally."

When I got back home at 8:00 p.m., Dion was there and was very ill. I, myself, had drank 3 glasses of wine; and I perceived I saw everything so clearly and proceeded to tell him so:

1) he didn't love me;
2) he always let me down;
3) I was out of compassion;
4) our marriage was a mistake.

He, already sick, became devastated. He nearly died in the night; was moaning and crying all night. He made several vomiting and bleeding trips to the bathroom; talking in his sleep; raving in Japanese and other languages.

Oddly, all I could feel was:

1) have another drink;
2) go ahead and die;
3) wonder what the Coroner's telephone number is.

April 13, 19_ - Monday

Today I went to the marriage counselor alone; then, took Dion to the VA Hospital. I honestly didn't believe he was going to live until we got there.

107

Everyone in the emergency room was busy and preoccupied, but they took one look at Dion and the waters parted. He looked like the sickest one in there. He was yellow, hunched over in his chair, and writhing in pain. Then, I began to feel compassion for him. A great sense of loss for all our golden moments unlived fell upon me.

I waited in the emergency room until they came out to tell me they were admitting him.

April 14, 19_ - Tuesday

After all the morning errands were done, I spent the rest of the day with Dion in intensive Care at the Hospital. When I walked in he looked as dead as I'd ever seen him; but, he was knocked out on Demerol.

Dion used to tell me, "Even when I am asleep, I can tell when you are in the room." When he would talk like this, I was reminded of the words to a Simon and Garfunkle song that went, " . .if they ever dropped the bomb, 'I'd find you in the flames."

Well, Dion must have been telling the truth because no sooner had I sat down by his bed than he opened his drugged, sleeping eyes and looked at me. He snapped totally awake and carried on a conversation with me.

In times like these, it becomes very apparent how really spiritual is Dion. He seems always to be one step ahead of me. He knows when I am near; knows when I am away. He knows what I am thinking; knows what I am about to do.

This phenomenon transcends mere intelligence. I know he has a high IQ; and, to quote my therapist, "even with half his brain cells dead from alcohol, his intelligence is still up there."

But, this "knowing" of his and my "knowing" in return is the stuff that dreams are made of. We are true soul mates. These unique occurrences are merely the evidence.

April 23, 19_ - Thursday

Dion, home from the hospital for a few days, is up to his old tricks again. Still sober, he ventured out today to go to Jessie's house to "finish up on the cars."

When he got home, I thought I could smell alcohol. I accused; he denied. Huge fight ensued. I know my behavior was wrong. I must go to Al-Anon Meetings.

April 24, 19_ - Friday

What was suspicion yesterday became fact today. Dion was sick again. He began to bleed; became nauseous.

The thing that astounds me in all this is JESSIE. Does she have absolutely no heart! How can she see him bleeding, dying, laying on his deathbed in the hospital and CONTINUE TO BUY HIM ALCOHOL! I realize that she isn't pouring the alcohol down his throat, but his blood is on her hands as surely as if she put poison in his food.

I have so many mixed feelings. Underneath everything, I am

108

seething. I seethe because Dion continues to cold-bloodedly murder himself. I seethe because he will not stay away from his accomplice. On top of that, I try to detach and "get on with my life."

Today we had planned to go fishing together. But, Dion still had cars to repair. He has customers waiting on their cars.

Jessie was out of town, so he masterminded for me to come over to her house so together we could hurry up and get the cars fixed and out of his hair.

While we worked side by side, I was aware that many of the side trips he sent me upon were so he could continue to sneak drinks purchased with the money Jessie gave him the first day out of the hospital. But strangely, I am only angry with myself that his so-called "deep love" isn't deeper than the addiction. Why am I angry with myself? I don't know. That is one of the mixed-up feelings I have tried to understand.

My last detour-errand was to get a Chilidog for Dion because he had begun to feel weak. As I drove back to Jessie's house, I did so just in time to see her pull into the drive with her daughter. Feeling sick in the pit of my stomach, I nevertheless, marched right up the driveway, head held high, no phony smiles, no words, looking deliberately the other way, snubbing them both.

The daughter looked at me as if she was ready to fight. Well, screw her AND her murdering, enabling Mother-Bitch.

April 26, 19_ - Sunday

Angry with Dion to the core, I prayed that God would take me away from him because he doesn't deserve me. Oddly enough, Dion said something to that effect last night while lamenting his drinking and putting his health in jeopardy.

He worked today at Jessie's until 6:00 p.m., when he called to say he was on the way home. He arrived at home at 9:00 p.m.

MAY TWO

May 1, 19_ - Friday

I have had to completely detach from expecting anything from Dion. To do otherwise, is to invite complete disappointment, then rage. From rage is born depression.

Monday, we fished at the lake. That was a nice, relaxing day; but, by Thursday, with my working the rest of the week, he had found a reason to go back over to Jessie's. Although he came home fairly early, he was ill the rest of the evening - yes, drinking.

Today when I got home from work at 4:00 p.m., he wasn't home. We had planned an evening of cooking on the grill because I brought the grandkids home with me to spend the night. Ordinarily, Dion LOVES being around the children, so I was very disappointed that he wasn't home.

I have no choice but to carry on as if he weren't coming home, as if his plans are often pipe dreams that may or may not happen.

May 7, 19_ - Thursday

This was supposed to be a week of "his taking care of his health," and "working at home;" and, in many ways it was exactly that.

Sunday, Dion tried to be sweet all day - and WAS. This time, I blew it with one hurtful remark that I am too ashamed to even write down. Oh, I could rationalize it away by saying that I am filled with rage for all the past year's worth of disappointments that I have had to swallow. But, to let myself off the hook like that is to avoid taking responsibility. After all, we can all find a way to justify our own destructive behavior. Dion somehow justifies his destructive drinking. Jessie obviously justifies her shameful predatory intrusions.

The result of my hateful remark was that Dion spent another fitful and unhappy night without sleep. I felt guilty all day Monday, but by then the damage was done.

Obviously, he set up something with Jessie for Tuesday, because when I came home, he was all dressed up. He met me on the stairs and said he felt guilty because he had done nothing around the house. He also looked hurt and VERY guilty when I said, "you got all dressed up for someone! You look wonderful." (He has begun to really let himself go lately, so this dressing up was truly a surprise.)

The phone rang; he didn't want to answer it, so we didn't. But, as soon as he left the house saying he was going to the "grocery store," I did *69 on the phone and found out that the call had come from a nearby restaurant. JESSIE!

So, I, up to my typical spy methods, followed him directly to the restaurant where the call came from; and yep, she was waiting.

Hiding in the bushes, I watched the place the entire time from the time they went into the restaurant until the time they came out. Sick, isn't it?

When they walked out, they didn't even walk out together. He had a very guilty look on his face; and, began to look around outside while she, no doubt, paid the tab. For a moment, I had the distinct feeling that Dion knew I was somewhere nearby.

When Jessie came out of the restaurant, she had that unhappy frown on her face. As they got into separate cars, there existed no physical contact between them of any kind whatsoever. There were no happy expressions. He looked like he couldn't WAIT to get away.

Once home he said he had spaced out and spent an hour confused and various and sundry other lies.

I didn't react because I felt numb.

Wednesday, he spent at home; did some drinking, but Jessie never called. Today, however, she called two times beginning at 2:00 p.m. We ignored the phone. He puttered around the house, acting like he didn't want to leave (though I could tell by his dress and the previous numerous and unanswered phone calls that he had plans).

Before he walked out the door, he remarked how peaceful it was sitting around with me. He said he hated to leave.

When he left at 6:00 p.m., he seemed torn and said he might just NOT work on the cars (please!); that he might get halfway to Jessie's and turn around and come back. I said, "That would be fine with me."

May 9, 19_ - Saturday

Friday, Dion "worked" at Jessie's. However, he had promised to be home at 4:30 p.m. to get the kids. And, he was true to his word even though Jessie was pissed at losing him so early, as evidenced by her annoyance at hearing my voice answer the phone.

May 10, 19_ - Sunday

Today Dion planned a special Mother's Day for me. He bought me a card that said:

"Once in a lifetime you find someone special,
And somehow you know this is the beginning
Of all you have longed for
A love you can build on, a love that will grow.
Once in a lifetime, to those who are lucky,
A miracle happens and dreams all come true.
I know it can happen; it happened to me,
For I've found that "once in a lifetime" with you.

Happy Mother's Day"

He signed it: *"Such a find!"*
"Not just a loving Mother, not just a loving Grandmother;
but, even in times of need, a Mother to me,
My life"

He had bought a bouquet of roses and had prearranged with a local Italian restaurant for them to stay open late just for us. We dined at 11:00

111

p.m. in the restaurant all by ourselves, which dinner he paid for!

After a pleasant day yesterday, Dion seemed to pick a fight to justify' going over to Jessie's; but, we worked it out. I went on to the therapist's. She isn't too happy with the non-progress between Dion and I; yet, he won't come to therapy with me.

May 12, 19_ - Tuesday

So, do I blame my therapist for my change of heart today? It happened like this: Dion arrived home last night at 12:18 p.m. For the millionth time, I was angry and felt abandoned. I could not find words to communicate with him. He doesn't seem to hear me; and, he says I don't hear him. So, I decided to talk no more. I suppose I took, to quote Dion's comment last July, "a vow of silence."

I found myself saying to him, "I want to return my life to its state before I met you." I admitted to him that I was aware that I have let him down many times; but, I said, "I am tired of the drinking; fearful of the lack of financial contribution; sick to death of Jessie's presence." I also told him that although I didn't feel he was really serious about sobriety, I knew it would take a huge effort to get rid of Jessie. I told him that I realize that I don't make him feel secure enough to cut the ties with Jessie. In saying this, I finally took responsibility for my contribution to all the times he has tried to exit himself from her presence only to have me let him down.

Our problem is very simple: Dion doesn't feel secure enough with me to cut ties with Jessie; and, I don't believe in him enough to relax my guard.

So tell me how I can love and miss him so. In his absence, I don't feel I tried hard enough to work on our marriage. I suspect he feels the same way. Each time we try again, he tries very hard. But, the tension builds and by the fifth day maximum, we are at each other's throats.

He said he would leave. Said that I could sell the van for money. He called Jessie early to pick him up.

May 19, 19_ - Tuesday

Exactly a week has passed, yet so much has happened.

Wednesday, May 13, Dion returned home only to sleep. He wouldn't communicate.

Thursday, May 14, he stayed with Jessie until way past midnight; yet, he still came home to sleep.

Friday, May 15, he went to the VA Hospital (Jessie drove him there). Yet, after his doctor's appointment, he came straight home and was STONE SOBER! Then it was that I softened and apologized for having been cruel to him; he apologized for "being a jerk."

Saturday, May 16, he, continuing on with his sobriety efforts, ignored Jessie's 40 million phone calls. We even enjoyed a light dinner together. When he is drinking he never eats; so, sharing meals together has become a small joy.

112

Sunday, May 17, we took a Sunday drive together. Later, we ordered in a pizza and ignored Jessie's every-thirty-minute phone calls.

Monday, May 18, we watched a very romantic movie together and shared a very romantic evening.

May 26, 19_ - Tuesday

The past week had been one of sobriety. Although there were relatively few ups and downs, today I experienced an anxiety attack similar to what a person on a tightrope might feel who looked down for a moment. I suppose you could say there has been tension between us all week that we both have worked hard to avoid.

I know I should lighten up and not worry about whether I say and do all of the right things. I should not focus on promises of sobriety, equality, and economic support. These are the sources of tension for me. I am not sure what causes Dion's tension, aside from the obvious one of trying not to drink.

Obviously all the feelings I had Dion had too, because today he went "back to work on cars" at Jessie's. He called late (7:00 p.m.), and I could tell he had resumed his drinking. He became angry when I hinted that Jessie was a murderer.

May 29, 19_ - Friday

My therapist has suggested that I journal, but not rag about Dion so much. So, although he has been a convenient scapegoat for my rage, I will attempt to focus the spotlight on me.

Today I found myself out shopping in an effort to fill up this void. I also began to fantasize about working more, saving money, buying another place, moving away from Dion.

The whole time I shopped, I felt guilty. A large part of me recognized that I had nothing to buy; that I was merely attempting to soothe the pain that I had avoided confronting for so many years.

I came home angry and did the obvious: I took it out on Dion. I said hateful things. I accused him of "making me do this, making me do that, keeping me from doing this, keeping me from doing that."

As long as I live I will never be able to forget the visual of Dion bending over as I spewed this awful rage. He bent over as if he were in physical pain; and, I believe he was.

For the first time ever, I have begun to agree with Jessie: I think I AM evil. I think I DO hurt people. WHAT IS WRONG WITH ME! WHAT HAS HAPPENED TO ME! I have become as addicted to cruelty as Dion is to alcohol. I watch these destructive patterns in myself, and, cannot find the trap door.

This evening was trauma filled. We were up all night fighting. Of course, after my tantrum yesterday, Dion left the house. He wouldn't stay to talk and resolve his hurt feelings. He left me all alone with nothing to fight with but the journal while he ran off to "Mama's" where he stayed until midnight.

I cannot give up now. I have a new resolve. I will try to speak positive sentences as often as possible. I will keep a record of good versus bad days each month and do a check and balance each month.

May 31, 19 - Sunday

Dion was in a strangely sad and honest state tonight. He was drunk; but, the shades fell away from my eyes and I saw a sad man, softhearted, socially unskilled, but trying to make it by.

Jessie is playing manipulator again. She has withheld money she owes him so he will have to come over each day to get it. Her scheme worked; they are at his favorite bar together (as they are most Sundays). But, tonight I don't feel angry with her. Matters are much too serious for that. Dion is near death and only a miracle can turn things around.

Oddly enough, Dion came home from the bar early enough to take us fishing. We fished so late into the evening that they locked the gates on us. We had to file off the locks to get out. Dion felt SO guilty about doing that even though we were just protecting ourselves so we could get home. That's the kind of sweetheart he really is.

JUNE TWO

June 1, 19_ - Monday

I decided to get a full time job (something I should have done long ago).

We need the money if there can ever be any hope of Dion breaking Jessie's money hold on him. Also, I need something else to give my attention to. It is necessary for me to find some area of success in my life so I won't put Dion under the gun all the time.

Dion began to sober up after an all night drinking spree with Jessie Sunday. I have a little concern about leaving him all alone each day five days a week while I work.

I asked him how he felt about me "abandoning him" by taking on a fill time job. His exact words were, "I'll get along." He said it with a little remorse; and, my immediate reaction was to feel guilty. But, I don't think he realizes how much he expects from me.

June 2, 19_ - Tuesday

As he often does when he attempts to quit drinking, Dion became very sick. This time, however, he developed trench mouth, which could be a reaction to the strong antibiotic the doctors gave him this last time he was there. But the trench mouth only adds to his agony because it makes eating extremely painful. And, heaven knows he needs to eat!

Presuming that all those phone calls that we didn't answer were Jessie calling, we ignored the phone.

June 3, 19_ - Wednesday

Dion had a very bad night. I feared he would die in the night. I think he felt this way too because he looked at me with fear in his big blue eyes and he said, "most drunks die on their third day of sobriety."

June 4, 19_ - Thursday

Dion was very weak and ill today. He said he couldn't feel his hands and feet; said his head felt funny.

Because I had to go to work, I buried the sword with Jessie long enough to ask her to sit with him while I worked. I truly feared he would die. My fear for Dion's well being overrides my intense disgust for Jessie. Naturally, she was all very eager to come rushing over.

When I called home at 5:00 p.m. to check on him, he said they were on their way to the hospital.

June 8, 19_ - Monday

The hospital didn't admit Dion, but they did give him prescriptions for his trench mouth. He has been lying around fairly listless all week while I have worked.

June 13, 19_ - Friday

I have worked all week. Dion has been so sick and going back and forth to the hospital that he hasn't had time or strength to drink.

He has become so incredibly irritable; and, I believe he is too ill to want to live.

Yesterday I said to him, "don't be afraid to die because you feel like a failure. If truth were told, you have given me the deepest feelings of love I have ever known. Your life has not been in vain, my love."

I can talk this way even though I know I would cry and cry if he did die. But, he has taught me something very valuable. After having taken care of him so well, I know that I can take care of myself.

Although there is no way we can ever be happy because he drinks, can't work, and won't even try to oust Jessie from our lives, I still love him very much. I have just given up hope that's all.

Saturday, June 14 - Dion spent the night at the hospital.

Sunday, June 15 - Dion came home and we spent a relatively peaceful and hostile-free day. Part of this was because I have tried to look at Dion as an individual and not as a bug to be dissected and examined. Also, when the phone began to ring incessantly today, Dion said, "unplug that damned phone."

Monday, June 16 - While I was at work, Jessie apparently CAME OVER, BARGED HER BUTT INTO OUR BUSINESS, AND TOOK DION OUT TO BUY GROCERIES AND CIGARETTES! I was so angry when I found this out, because although he had been doing much better, he was sick again after their two-hour grocery-shopping outing. I'm sure she made certain he had, "something to make you feel better," (her infamous quote when she wants to get him started drinking again).

Alcohol and money are the only holds Jessie has on Dion; and, she is going to kill him for her own selfish purposes. She has long since figured out he doesn't have too much in common with her when he is attempting sobriety.

When I got home, I said, "Dion, WHY do you think I am working? I am working so we can buy all the groceries and cigarettes you need! We don't need Jessie's CIGARETTE AND GROCERY money!"

Tuesday, June 17, and Wednesday, June 18, Dion was home when I got home from work. The answering machine was FULL of messages from Jessie. It was obvious that neither did he answer the phone all day, nor did he bother to check the messages.

I can really see that he is trying to separate himself from Jessie; but, since he is trying to do it without confrontation or without hurting her feelings, he isn't driving home the message too well.

I have been "holding my breath," because with her out of the picture, he has managed, with relative ease, to accomplish a 19-day sobriety. He was beginning to feel much better.

June 23, 19_ - Tuesday

Tonight we watched <u>The People vs Larry Flint</u>. How I identified with that movie.

Dion and I have spent most of our life together cloistered inside behind closed doors most mornings and afternoons up until 4:00 p.m. (his usual departing time).

Another parallel regarding that couple and Dion and I are our intense devotion to one another despite problems and roadblocks that we both ignore and make the best of. Granted, the loss of normalcy in my own life doesn't even come close to Larry Flint's wife's tremendous descent into drugs. But, in my own way, I feel as out of control as she looked; yet, I still love Dion deeply - almost like a wounded hound who has no where else to go (although many people, family members included, tell me this isn't so).

Dion has for the most part, behaved beautifully while I have worked full time. There is no one more surprised than I. However, I think the main reason for this is because he is too sick to act otherwise.

June 28, 19_ - Sunday

Somewhere between the time I began to brag on Dion and today, Jessie managed to worm her way back in (while I was working); and, one day along that time, he left the serenity of our home and went to her house. He has had a drink every day since then; and, although I cannot remember exact dates, he really descended rapidly (emotionally) on Thursday after a "fight" with her over something.

I don't know the gist of their fight. I only recognized that they were fighting when I played back the answering machine message where she had said, "Dion, if what I said wasn't true, why did you hang up on me? And, you didn't call back to check on me after I was taken to the emergency room...... because YOU DON'T care." Then she said, "Okay! G-O-O-D-B-Y-E!"

Needless to say, he has treated me like crap since the day I discovered the message. I didn't let him know that I had heard the message. I did, however, attempt to point out to him that Jessie is coming between us by jeopardizing his serenity, his sobriety, and his attempt to regain his physical health.

Feebly, I attempt to get on with my life. I have lost contact with all friends. My wardrobe has slipped so (from poverty) that when I go to work I depend on "clever jewelry" to detract from my threadbare clothes (most of them were already threadbare when I bought them, since I tend to shop at second hand stores).

Dion's latest complaint is that I don't involve him in my life at all. At first, this new complaint created guilt in me because my embarrassment over him is an absolutely correct observation. But, when I think back, I remember that I have on numerous occasions invited him to accompany me everywhere. I think I gave up inviting him anywhere after he disappointed me this past Easter Sunday. Also, in looking back, I seem to remember that he has usually declined my invitations. I think he just notices this new void because he has finally made a conscious effort to get rid of Jessie. She isn't there to "take up the slack" in his life.

He also complained that I was never home anymore. Poor Dion, he is reaping the harvest of my decision to create a new, working outlet for myself because I was going crazy being home all the time while he was out all hours drinking. Someone here has closed the gate AFTER the horse got out.

Sad, sad, sad. I am at such a loss to know how to make him happy.

JULY TWO

July 4, 19__ - Saturday

Although Dion has always found reasons to berate me, in more lucid moments he has admitted, "our fight is only about one thing: I am sick; and you are healthy."

This last episode of fighting dates back to June 16 and Dion's involvement with Jessie. The primary issue is this: there is no man beneath Dion's flesh. A demon lives in Dion's place.

When I hear these new accusations from Dion of how, "you don't involve me in your life," or "you don't spend time with me," or "you just want to get away from me," or "you are pulling away from me," or "you have another life," and all other such guilt-inducing snippets, I just want to give up.

July 5, 19_ - Sunday

We spent a very uneventful 4th as Dion clung to life and Jessie called 5 million times a day. Regarding the ringing phone, we always do the same thing (ignore the calls); and Jessie always leaves the same message on the answering machine: "Dion"   (long pause as if Dion plans to pick up the phone when he hears it is she) "Jessie". . (another long pause)…. "just calling to see how you are" (you should know, bitch, as you freely supply the poison that kills him)… "give me a call."….. (yeah, right!).

Dion has said that even the sound of her voice makes him want to drink. Yesterday, after the phone rang the third time (only once did she leave a message, the other two were hang-ups), Dion yelled at the phone, "SHUT UP!"

He says she is ugly. He says that she stands for everything he hates: "religious hypocrisy and sanctimonious bullshit."

The last time I went to Jessie's house to pick up Dion, she told me to get off her property or she would call the police. I told her, "I am here to pick up my husband."

Why do I go over and over this vile crap in my head?

July 12, 19__ - Sunday

Monday, I took Dion to the hospital to get water tapped off his stomach (a condition of ascites).

Tuesday, I saw my therapist.

Wednesday, Dion had a drink and began to go downhill.

Thursday, Jessie moved in via phone calls while I worked all day. Needless to say, Dion slipped more.

Friday, Dion watched my grandson while I worked. My heart began to "act up."

Saturday, Jessie called and after the answering machine came on, she left the phone off the hook and used up all of the 30-minute tape.

Saturday night I had what I believe to be a slight heart attack. Dion woke me in the middle of the night asking for orange juice. I said I was too sick to move. He got up and got himself watermelon.

Today, he woke me up at 7:30 a.m. and raged all morning in pain. He was vomiting old dark blood. Even his stool was stained with old dark blood. It became evident to me that he was bleeding internally. I gave him three pain pills, knowing they would probably further damage his condition but not as much as the drinks Jessie bought him yesterday.

I don't know how much longer I can hold up under this pressure. The demon that threatens to "take Dion out," threatens to take me out too.

July 14, 19_ - Tuesday

I had to depend on Jessie again to take Dion to the emergency room while I worked. He was vomiting massive amounts of blood this morning.

Once he was admitted to the hospital, Jessie called me at work (Dion had given her the number to tell me how he was) and began to "gossip" about Dion. She started telling me all the things he supposedly told her.

You might say that I violated rule number one in the art of war: I listened to the enemy.

I must say this: if the great manipulator knew how to manipulate Dion, she certainly knew how to manipulate me too. She said something that stopped me cold in my tracks. She said Dion said that we weren't married. Then she backtracked a little and said Dion told her we were married; but, that I had "tricked" him into marriage with a piece of paper drawn up by some lawyer.

I SAW RED! I began to question myself; began to doubt Dion. Did he really tell her this? Did he really feel "tricked" into marriage?

The result of this "little confidential conversation" accomplished exactly what it was intended to accomplish! I went straight home and packed up every item that belonged to Dion and shoved it out the front door. Jessie was all too happy to come and pick it up (she made several trips back and forth to take it over to her house).

My anger and uncertainty about Dion endured all through several phone calls initiated by Dion and executed by the emergency room nurse asking me when I planned to "visit my husband."

To add fuel to the fire, I told Jessie to go tell Dion that I had moved his stuff out and that I would be filing for divorce. My exact words to Jessie were, "if he felt that I tricked him into marriage, he certainly shouldn't mind a divorce."

July 15, 19__ - Wednesday

Jessie visited Dion today in the emergency room, but didn't tell him I had left him. I understand from Jessie's second-hand information that he became extremely angry with her because she wouldn't stay with him all day at the hospital.

All of his things are moved out. Jessie calls me each night to "gossip." Everything she tells me hurts like crazy. Finally I told her, "I don't want to discuss Dion anymore. You have him; that's what you have wanted. I don't have strength to continue to drone on about this."

However, she still calls each night. I am on the verge of unplugging the phone. I am beginning to believe she is senile.

July 17, 19_ - Friday

I have cooled down and realized with great anguish the damage I have done. I feel SO guilty about reacting to the words (probably lies) of Jessie, the Enemy that I have not been able to stop sobbing. It had taken Dion and I almost one year to get set up in our cozy little home; and, I banished it in one afternoon. I almost feel I have gone too far this time.

Today, I could stand the pain of separation no longer; and, went to the hospital to visit Dion. He looked so small in his bed; he looked so sad. But, more than anything else, he looked puzzled when he saw me. His first comment was, "I never know what you are going to do."

I wanted to say the same thing back to him. However, I said nothing to him because I could not find words. I tried talking to him, but the enormity of my betrayal seemed impassable.

I did relate all of the things Jessie had told me. He denied each one. He said, "I cannot believe you give her so much power. She is nothing."

I wanted to scream, "if she is nothing why do you give her the power to take your life?"

This was the direction of our conversation; this was the impasse over which we both seemed incapable of rising above. We parted on sweet terms, however. Why shouldn't we? We both love each other deeply? We just haven't been able to find the key to getting along with one another.

Pain again stabbed my heart when I rose to leave because I realized that Dion was saying goodbye (something he had NEVER BEFORE AGREED TO SAY) when he said, "take care of yourself, little one."

July 19, 19_ - Sunday

Today I went again to visit Dion in the hospital. This time, though, I felt it especially difficult to talk with him. I found it hard to make him understand how I had become so weary of putting myself last while I catered to him hand and foot. I tried to make him understand that in order for our marriage to work, I needed for him to try also. I needed for him to meet me halfway. I needed for him to get Jessie out of our lives.

July 20, 19_ - Monday

I went to the hospital after work. This time we argued about getting back together. I tried to make him understand that as much as I loved him, there needed to be huge changes made. I again expressed dismay at all the "gossip" that dropped from Jessie's lips.

He said something that shocked me. He said, "I thought we were getting along, honey. I thought you were happy."

If this is true, he must feel extremely bewildered and betrayed by my moving him out.

He said, "when I get out of here I WILL NOT live with Jessie. If you don't want me to come back home, we'll have to find another place for me to live. But, I will not live with Jessie. I hate the thought of being over there."

These are the types of things about Dion that make me crazy. I ask myself if he hates being over there WHY DOES HE SPEND SO MUCH TIME OVER THERE? Yet, my heart knows the answer: he is addicted to alcohol. He goes over there to drink; and, she waves his weakness in front of his nose like a big piece of bait.

July 22, 19_ - Wednesday

Tonight after work I visited Dion in the hospital. When I went into the room, he held out his hand. I took his hand. He gestured for me to sit down. I pulled up a chair and sat beside his bed holding his hand.

He said, "I have been thinking about you all evening. How delicate you are. I'm going to try and give you what you need because I love you very, very much."

I asked him what he meant by "… give you what you need... alcohol rehabilitation?"

He said, "I'll look at that too."

July 23, 19_ - Thursday

Jessie called me at work today to tell me that she had brought Dion home. She went on in that excited schoolgirl voice which tells me she is delighted to have him there despite all the horrible things she said about him earlier in the week.

But, I am too exhausted to care about her and her ramblings. I continue to mourn the man I love. I mourn the memory of kisses in the rain, lovemaking on the beach in the tent. My vision is of that sexy guy with the long blonde hair peeking out from under his black hat. He played and sang on stage so beautifully that a girl once tried to pick him up. He told the girl he was engaged to be married (this was while I was still refusing to marry him).

He had put it into his mind, even back then, that we were engaged; and, no amount of hedging on my part would discourage him from believing this.

I am GLAD, now, that he was so positive about our marriage becoming a reality. I am GLAD I married him and, "made an honest man out of him." My love for him makes me proud to call myself his wife.

July 24, 19_ - Friday

It is two days away from my 52nd birthday; and, I feel so bad I feel I could die. Exhausted, weak and unable to catch my breath, I think my heart is acting up. But, I must keep going long enough to get out of debt. I cannot afford to be sick.

Dion called me today from Jessie's and asked if I would take him

122

tomorrow to the VA Social Worker to check into the alcohol in-house treatment. I said I would.

When I picked Dion up today to take him to check into alcohol rehab, I couldn't help but notice how frail he looked. He has a pall to him that I never noticed before. He has a tremble, an almost faltering walk, as if it is difficult for him to put one foot in front of the other.

I love him like I have loved no man. Although the Dion today hardly resembles the fun, handsome, exciting, dynamic, sexy guy he was, my love has nothing to do with how he looks. I looked at him in this failing, tender manner and my heart saw only the man I love. I truly love his spirit. My eyes are blind.

After his interview with the social worker, she called me into her office separately. She told me that based on his talk with her, she felt that he had a very slim chance for rehabilitation. Although I had long suspected that Dion could be labeled an "incurable alcoholic," this was the first time I had ever heard a professional confirm my suspicions.

However, my secret doubts didn't stop me from saying to her, "I didn't think you people ever gave up on addicts. I thought you maintained that there was always hope."

She said something like, "that is true if the person has hit bottom and really wants to change."

I've always known my Dion was strong and stubborn. Oddly enough, this same strength that has helped him to defy death several times has also prevented him from admitting defeat long enough to reach out and ask for help.

I said to the social worker, "all we can do is try. I cannot give up on him; although, I am ashamed to admit that I have moved him out of the house. So, maybe deep down, I have given up on him."

July 26, 19__ - Sunday

Today is my birthday; and, I have spent it alone. But, that isn't Dion's fault.

Yesterday, after I dropped Dion off at Jessie's after our unsuccessful meeting with the social worker, he called me later to tell me that he wanted to spend my birthday with me.

When I called back today to tell him I was on my way over to pick him up, Jessie answered the phone. I said, "I am coming over to pick up Dion."

She then related to me how angry she was with him because he had convinced her last night to go to Sears saying he wanted some tools. She said she gave him the credit card; then followed him to the jewelry department where it became obvious to her that he was going to buy some jewelry.

Then the bitch said, "I figured he was going to buy you some jewelry to BUY YOU OFF (whatever that means)."

I told her, "Today is my birthday. I suspect he wanted to buy me a

123

present."

When she heard this, she went through the roof. She really screamed.

I said, "Jessie, sounds like you are saying it was okay for him to use your card to buy himself tools; but, you didn't want him buying me a present."

She yelled, "Would you?" Then she slammed the phone down; and, I know I will not be seeing Dion tonight.

Why, oh why did I desert my beloved? I have always had huge doubts about his well being in her care. But, all along it has been up to Dion to extradite himself from Jessie's presence completely. I cannot tolerate Jessie between us anymore even if it is just for him to use her.

July 29, 19_ - Wednesday

This week marks the milestone of a real turning point in the lives of Dion and I. It is now after all these months, after all the trauma that has transpired between us, that we have REALLY BEGAN TO COMMUNICATE.

Monday, I met with Dion in the park behind Jessie's house. Although Jessie acted like my friend in communicating to me all those "things" Dion said (lies she concocted), she has now turned the tables and won't let me come to her house to see him anymore. So, she has proven herself to be the snake I always deep in my heart knew her to be.

When I saw him sitting on the park bench, my heart went out to him. I have missed him so. There is a huge gap gone out of my life. I have loved him far more than ever I realized. God gave him to me; and, I didn't appreciate him.

He said some very sobering things Monday. He recapped our whole devastating relationship beginning with how when we met we were "married in heart and spirit." But, he feared I was miserable the day we got married. He said he was proud of my progress since he has been out of my life.

Dion said his life's greatest accomplishment was "our little marriage." He said he didn't see us living together again. I sobbed like never before.

Tuesday, he said he wanted to talk with me more. When I asked if he was coming back, he said he didn't know. He said, "sometimes when you really love someone the best thing you can do is to let them go." He said he was married to a beautiful woman and he would be happy with that. He said he had done a lot of thinking about his Dad and G_____: how they loved each other, yet maintained two separate residences because they fought like we did.

Tonight (actually it is early Wednesday morning) my heart is broken. I feel so lost and like such a failure. I am a ghost of a woman going through life's motions, needing Dion's love, still lonely, still grieving, having thrown a perfectly wonderful man to the wolves.

Interestingly enough, Dion's new detachment makes me aware of how much I used his deep love of me to control him. I gave him this message, "do this.. ..do that... .quit this… quit that.... or you're out of the picture."

What I find underneath the mystery of who is Dion (or better known for universal purposes as who is this man in my life) is a deep loneliness. I find deep needs to connect; but, an inability to do so satisfactorily. He tried loving me; I rejected him. Now that he has gone; I need him. The pain of aloneness and rejection is incredible. Yes, it is a replay of my lonely childhood, but guilt and a bruised ego have been added.

I even allowed the enemy to take my love from me. So, stupidity on my part even enters the picture. Just like a charm, Jessie moved in, told some lies, and I believed her. Now that she has Dion living back in her house, she has blatantly dumped me; has no more concern for my welfare; and even looks oddly dressed and perfumed up when I go over there.

Regardless of the reason for Dion's sudden spiritual strength, one thing is obvious. I no longer have control of the situation. I cannot force order onto this. I have no choice now but to give up.

Dion also said one thing with regard to Jessie that makes a lot of sense. I am wondering if he has just realized this or if he has known it all along. If the latter is the case, I wonder why he didn't communicate this to me while we were still together and in the heat of the battle.

He said, "we need to work to make our marriage strong. Then you will have no need to go running to your kid's for support; and, I will have no need to go running to Jessie for support. We need to learn how to support one another."

July 30, 19_ - Thursday

Dion and I talked on the phone last evening. He made me aware how much I must listen to him. He talked of getting a job and stopping drinking. He talked of getting his own place to live.

Later in the evening when I called him, he said he would call me back on the other phone - still hiding from Jessie. He also sounded like he is drinking heavy again.

July 31, 19__ - Friday

When I talk with Dion, it is obvious to me that he believes I was miserable with him. I think my mistake was in believing that his actions needed changing rather than deciding: this is Dion. Love him for all his faults.

AUGUST TWO

August 1, 19_ - Saturday

Dion was supposed to spend this evening with me and see the kids. To hear Jessie tell it, she is tired of his furious temper. To hear Dion tell it, she is very rude to him. Reading between the lines, I would guess that he mentioned to her that he was going to spend the evening with me. Then probbly got angry and then he became "furious."

I am sure that Jessie is rude to Dion. She obviously knows by now that his moving back to her house had everything to do with my throwing him out and nothing to do with his interest in her. She is, by now, obviously forced to accept her true function in Dion's life: that of enabler.

All of us creatures who listen to our hearts know the truth. Some of us learn that fighting against the truth does not make it change. One of the reasons that Jessie continued to wear Dion down with her fighting was because she was hell bent on forcing him to admit things to her that were not truths.

She <u>knew</u> deep in her heart that we were married, but she didn't want to accept it. She <u>knew</u> deep in her heart that Dion and I were soulmates, yet she tried with all her might to change destiny.

Putting pettiness aside and attempting to pick Dion up from her house so we could spend the evening together, I called over there, but there was no answer. I decided to let drop the planned evening out. He had already discussed with me over the phone the tense atmosphere that existed over there. I didn't want to cause Dion ANY MORE STRESS THAN NECESSARY.

Dion called me at 11:00 p.m. to apologize for letting me down. He said he was afraid of me; he felt out-classed by me; he said he was afraid to even entertain the hope that we could resume our "happy" life.

The irony in this is that we didn't have what most people would call a "happy" life. We had love and deep spiritual union. We were created to be together, but we never managed to find peace. However, in our defense, I will say this: we always continued to try to find a way to find that peace together.

I tried to communicate my feelings honestly with Dion. I told him that I didn't feel we had had a "happy" life together. I raised the concern that he had spent more time with Jessie than with me, I also raised the hurtful issue that he denied to her that we were married. He swore she lied about that.

By the end of our conversation, Dion became so choked up with tears that I could hardly understand him.

After my conversation with Dion, I called his Mother, who is in a two-hour time difference, so it wasn't quite 9:30 p.m. where she lived. She said she had always felt that Jessie was a wicked, selfish woman.

She maintained that Dion's sobriety was and would continue to be greatly sabotaged as long as he had someone giving him money.

I called Dion at 2:00 p.m. today to see if we still had plans for tonight and he said yes. But, when I called him back to say I was on the way to pick him up, he sounded extremely groggy and said wait another hour.

I called back in an hour. Jessie answered. I said, "I am coming over to pick up Dion so we can visit the kids."

She said, "Well, he has gotten real sick."

I asked, "Has he had a drink?"

She answered without conviction, "No." Then she offered this bright ray of hope, "I don't think he is going to make it. I think he is going to die."

My insides began screaming at her: WHAT THE <u>HELL</u> DO YOU CARE! YOU WOULD LOVE TO SEE HIM DIE SINCE YOU HAVE REALIZED YOUR VAPIDITY IN HIS

REGARD.

But, all I said was, "Well, Jessie, you have been negative since day one."

I slammed down the phone and wanted to run out into the streets like a mad woman screaming, "Someone help me! My husband is being held hostage by a bottle of alcohol and a manipulative, jealous woman and it's all my fault because instead of loving him unconditionally when I had the chance, I set limits, played games, threatened, scorned, shamed, blamed, rejected, pouted.   And, furthermore, when my beloved was at his low point, I threw him out!"

Why have I not plastered I Corinthians 13:4-7 on my heart and behaved accordingly? Why did I, throughout countless therapist sessions, continue to live in denial, therefore making the problem worse? Why did I not continue to attend Al Anon until I understood what I so need to understand now; that, not everything is within my control; sometimes things just are; only God understands all things.

August 3, 19__ - Monday

Last night I went over to Jessie's and picked up Dion anyway. He was in a very sullen, downtrodden, non-communicative mood. I fought discouragement because the plan had been for him to spend the night with me and we would make plans to get back together.

In an attempt to interrupt the usual argument cycle that Dion and I manage to perpetuate, which usually begins with him long-faced and with me questioning him about his mood, I decided to adopt the Buddhist dying man fable where on the dying man's plunge to death, he stops to enjoy a strawberry. In order to do this one must cherish the moment for whatever small thing one can find to cherish.

My first observation about Dion when I picked him up was that Jessie had again lied. She said he had not had a drink. He had! She also

127

said his color looked bad; that he was dying. Wrong! He had color. He looked good.

But, tonight for some strange reason I decided to adopt the Al Anon slogan: Live and Let Live, or translated into Buddhist terms: embrace the moment.

So, there we were - Dion, staring blankly out of the car window, me - unsure what to do or say. In this mode it was that we drove to a Chinese Restaurant.

At the restaurant, Dion ordered Egg Drop soup and ate heartily. He began to feel better. He looked at something across the room and smiled. This was the first smile of the evening; and it was a very engaging smile, very sincere. I turned around to look at what made him smile. Behind me was a large fish tank, which contained brightly colored fish that swam between fake, plastic seaweed.

"I was looking at that beautiful yellow fish," Dion said.

"Is he a gold fish?" I asked.

"No," said Dion. "That fish is the color of the sun." And, truly, he was. The fish was fairly large and was the color of a bright, yellow sun.

"That fish reminds me," said Dion, still smiling, "Of one of those ancient inscriptions where creatures represented words. You know," he said, " when the sun was a winged bird."

"What ancient inscriptions?" I asked. "Do you mean the hieroglyphics on the walls of the Egyptian tombs?"

"Ancient," said Dion, "Before Aphrodite."

The tension between us broken, we passed the rest of the meal in loving peace. He agreed to call me tomorrow as soon as I got home from work.

August 4, 19_ - Tuesday

I got home early from work today, so I called Jessie's house. I was hoping that Dion would answer; however, Jessie did. I told her that Dion and I had decided last night that he would be moving back in with me. I told her I was on my way over to pick up some of his things.

She said, "He is real sick right now. I am trying to get him to go to the hospital."

After we hung up the phone, it rang again within two minutes. Jessie obviously couldn't wait to call me back and lay this message on me, "He said he doesn't give a damn about what we want. He said he would never come back over there and climb those stairs again. He said he was dying...."

So, I get the message. When she heard from me that Dion would be moving back, she hung up the phone, quizzed him about it, and then called me back with her two counterfeit cents. What can I do? What power do I have? I have none. I was the fool who threw a fit and moved him back over to her house in the first place. These are the consequences I must suffer for being so impetuous and immature where someone's life in concerned.

Dion called me back later in the evening. He sounded very weak - almost too weak to talk. He said that since our talk on Sunday about him coming back "home" he has fresh hope for us becoming a family again. He said his only fear now is the fear that he might not be able to get his health back.

This sounded to me to be quite a different story than Jessie's claim that he said, "I am dying. I just wish you and Rose would leave me alone."

Dion kept lamenting about how after giving Jessie back all the musical equipment pieces, that we had lost all the ground it took us a year to gain. Some tiny voice inside me fears this might be too high a mountain for Dion to climb to get back his health and fight Jessie to get the musical equipment back into our possession.

I made a mistake by acting hastily out of anger and rage. I played the art of war very wrong. Jessie had been trying to get back all of the "stuff" the entire time Dion and I were together; but, he was strong then and had enough fight in him to defend both of us against her.

August 5, 19___ - Wednesday

Dion called me late last night. He was so weak he could barely talk. He said he is on his second day of sobriety. He said that since we talked on Sunday, he believed we could make it together this time. I told him that although I knew I loved him, I never knew how much I loved him until he was gone from here. I also told him I had never realized how much I needed him. Life is completely empty without him.

It was true. After all his things were moved out, the first thing I did was to clean and redecorate everything the way I had always wanted it to be. Suddenly, his absence began to loudly announce itself to me. Here I sat in a house that resembled a clean museum. I didn't "live" in the house the same way we did when Dion was here. I didn't turn on as many lights. The kitchen became a virtual microwave room. His bathroom, absent his shave mug, sat clean and all tidied up sporting a phony, painted wood fish in the place where his mug had once been. All the ashtrays in the house were clean. I had put an ashtray in each room for him. There was one big one in the living room. There were two ashtrays in the kitchen because he loved to cook; and did most of the cooking. There was also one in his bathroom; one in my bathroom; one by our bed; and one in his workroom.

He couldn't talk long. He said he missed me and loved me. He said he was afraid of going through the third day of sobriety alone (or in Jessie's non-care) and he promised me that he would check himself into the hospital tomorrow.

Before we hung up the phone, he asked me, "What should I eat?"

I said, "she isn't taking good care of you, is she."

He said he hadn't taken any of his medicine. I told him to take the Thiamin and Folic Acid for sure. I suggested he should drink orange juice, eat soup, and eat an egg and toast later. I said, "Try to eat every two hours. Also, get up and walk around the room."

He said he couldn't walk; he was too weak.

I told him how helpless I felt with him being over there. I said it seemed strange that my husband was living in another woman's house. He agreed.

He said he missed me. He voiced concern that he, "might not make it." I told him he would make it. "When you get well this time," I said, "We will begin with walks so you can get your strength back. I am not giving up on you," I said. " Never."

This morning Jessie called to say he is some better. No kidding! Maybe he has decided he wants to live and has quit drinking the booze you make so available.

I will NEVER AGAIN give up on my beloved. Nor will I fight over him again. He was correct in saying that the closer he and I became, the more Jessie would be phased out.

August 6, 19_ - Thursday

Dion called late last night sounding very weak. He said he couldn't talk long. He obviously called while Jessie was asleep because he spoke freely about missing me and loving me. He said he hoped he would make it. He said his fight was gone. I told him if he could hang on four more months, we could celebrate one year of marriage. That seemed to cheer him up a lot.

This morning Jessie called to spread her "sour" cheer. She said we were both crazies for putting up with Dion. (Speak for yourself, stupid.)

"We're both sick," she said.

"Not me," I said, now getting very angry.

But, I didn't have the guts to say the rest of what I was thinking: 'you are the one who bought him drink after drink because it was the only way you could get him to spend time with you. Blood is on your hands, Lady. Don't point your bony, murdering finger at me!'

Then she got around to the real purpose of her call. She said, "I told Dion, you need to get better so you can be with your wife. And, he said, I don't care about her. I just care about getting my health back."

All the while she was rambling on, I was thinking, "Can't you spare me any hope? Can you convey no good news? Must you, even in Dion's death continue to deny his love of me? Is your ego such that you must continue to rag on a dying man about his marriage to another woman? And what a pitiful creature you are that you should be so eager to call a dying man's wife up just to convey to her that his last words were: I don't care about her."

August 7, 19_ - Friday

True to his word, Dion checked himself into the hospital yesterday. I waited all day to hear from someone about how he was doing. Finally, when I got home from work, I called the hospital and located him in the

Intensive Care Unit.

I was able to talk to the doctor. I told him that Dion was still drinking. He was shocked! I told him Jessie would continue to give him money; would even take him out to visit his favorite bars and restaurants so he could continue drinking. Even the doctor became angry. He couldn't believe it and said, "this is NOT good news."

I have done some research and found a place where Dion can go for in-patient treatment. Regarding the cost: they haven't said, but said they would work with us.

I went this morning to the hospital to see Dion. He seemed surprised to see me. He said he felt a thousand percent better today. Although he faded in and out from painkillers and sleeping pills, that sharp intellect was still in tact. He kept up his end of the conversation very well.

He can look in my eyes and know what I am thinking. Once he said, "Now, you can't be afraid of me, you hear?"

Once when the nurse asked me to take off a bandage in five minutes, I looked at Dion and said, "He ain't heavy; he's my hubby." He smiled because he knew what I meant. He got my humor.

Once he said, "they're not gonna lick us, kid," and when I left he asked when I would be back.

I said, "You need not worry, my love, I will never desert you as I once did." He said he loved me.

August 8, 19_ - Saturday

I haven't been to the grocery store in the three weeks that Dion has been gone except to buy milk and cat food. At first, I ate the frozen leftovers. Then, I ate the bread. Then, I prepared some boxed pasta we had. Mostly, I have lost my appetite.

I find lying beneath my addiction to changing Dion is my own malignant loneliness.

August 9, 19__ - Sunday

Tonight is a classic example of what drives me crazy about Dion. I visited him in the hospital, now seven days sober. After I settled in, he asked me in a very low and unemotional tone of voice, "Do you love me? You don't have to lie to me anymore."

I said, "I've only been telling you for two weeks now how I've loved and missed you. Why? Do you really love me?"

He didn't answer, so in the interest of an attempt at keeping things light, I let it drop.

Next he said, "You look like a million bucks," which usually is followed by comments such as "who are you dressing up for?" However, he omitted that part.

I replied, "Are you saying you love me?"

He said, "No. I'm saying you look like a million bucks."

I said, "Thank you,"

His next pointed remark was designed to highlight the pain he felt by my moving him out of the house. He said, "So, what do you plan to do around your place?"

"Nothing," I said. "Besides, don't call it <u>my place.</u>"

He said, "Are you going to sand and refinish the cabinets?

"No," I said.

"Why don't you just sand and re-stain the cabinets instead of painting them?" he asked.

"Because the cabinets aren't real wood," I say. "They are particle board. They will look better just painted."

"Yes dear," he said. Then he said, "I should know not to try and tell you what to do around your place."

"Dion," I said, "I don't want you to feel that way. Now, I feel guilty."

"Why," he said, "I have no right to tell you what to do in your own house."

"I feel guilty," I said, "because I don't want you to think your opinions don't matter."

"You've lived life the way you wanted it so long, it is hard to change," he said.

"But, we are married now," I said. "Things are different."

Then he said something about not having the right to interfere; and, I said he makes me feel like I'm out here by myself. "Sounds to me," I said, "like you don't want to be a part of my life."

He said I was leading the conversation into places he didn't intend to go.

"No," I said, "I just hear you saying you don't want to be a part of my life anymore. I don't think you love me."

"Why do you think that," he asked.

"Because I have no evidence of it," I said. "You don't try to take care of me. You didn't commit to me; not really," (meaning Jessie).

Then he said how he couldn't make me happy. And, I think, "No, you work very hard at making me miserable."

August 10, 19_ - Monday

Dion called late last night to say he couldn't go to sleep knowing I left unhappy. I thanked him for calling (he didn't actually apologize for picking a fight, yet his call was something of an unspoken one). I told him I loved him. He said he loved me in a low, rushed way as if he regretted saying it.

This morning he called to ask how I was. Naturally, I let fly all my fears, questions, anxieties. He twisted my words all around and ended with, "I just called to ask how you are; and, to ask if you are coming today."

I apologized for voicing my fears (to someone who, by his actions, does not give a flip).

In an attempt to remember that love is an action, a commitment to concern and kindness, I will try to quit asking for anything from him. His obvious resentment toward me goes deep - too deep to gloss over with sweet words and futile apologies.

Counseling is in order; yet he refuses. Hopefully, I can back off and love myself. The trick is to do so without resentment.

August 11, 19__ - Tuesday

Big Jessie mystery: where is she? When I arrived at the hospital yesterday around 2:30 p.m., Dion had mellowed. Later in the day it became clear why he was so concerned that I come to the hospital: Jessie has been absent for two days.

He said she was in the _____ hospital. He said she had had a heart attack. I called the _____ hospital. She was not there; nor had she been admitted. I called her house. Someone besides Jessie answered. Said Jessie would be back today. So, who is telling whom what?

Meanwhile, Dion, a candidate for a liver shunt is clearly not the Dion I know. He is very reserved, cold. He warms to me slowly each day.

These past few months have been a lesson in maturity, as I cope without escape hatches in a hostile world devoid of "mommy" substitutes. Had I matured in my late 20's as most normal people do, I might have put my intelligence to use by becoming a professional. As it is, I move in mundane circles and mistake my intelligence for neurosis.

August 13, 19__ - Thursday

When I called Dion at the hospital this morning, he was obviously very full of resentment, still. I decided to comment on his pouting behavior by saying, "I feel we have lost something."

He said, "we never see each other." Then he reminded me that it has been nearly a month since I threw him out. Before that, he pointed out I was working non-stop. What angered me here was his complete disregard that I DO work. Also, it angered me that while I had been to the hospital Saturday, Sunday, Monday, he said we never saw each other.

I couldn't talk to him because he accused me of 'playing games.' Communication seemed to have completely stopped. I hung up the phone thinking: screw him - I won't go to the hospital.

He called me back. He said the key words, "I'm too sick for resentment." Maybe I am the self-centered one who fails to see truth.

So, once and for all, I went to the hospital tonight. I walked into the room and said, "Dion, what is wrong?"

I sat on a chair by his bed and didn't say another word. He had often accused me of not listening. Tonight I decided I would not be guilty of not listening. I would be quiet and really listen.

He said he was afraid that I had been leading another life. He asked me why I was being so quiet.

133

I sat there sincerely pondering his question. I said, "Dion, our entire time together, you have accused me of never listening to you. Perhaps you were right. I believe that I often talk instead of listen because I mistakenly believe that as long as I am talking, I am in control. But, who wants to be in control of a one-way street? All I really want from you is your love and our life together. I came into this relationship with all my fears gathered around me like fat sacks of flour. I was afraid of you and of your strength and of your ability to hurt me. I was afraid of your drinking problem. I tried to tear you apart and put you back together my way. I tried to turn you into someone I wouldn't be afraid of. But, in doing so, I left a very valuable package behind - you. I almost annihilated the Dion that I loved. It is obvious to me now that I have no more answers. I must listen to you if I am to find you again."

Our evening in the hospital ended very warmly and sweetly. I sat by the bed late into the night as he dozed and woke back up. He looked at me once when he woke up and said, "This is the thing I like most: being with you and doing quiet things together."

August 14, 19__ - Friday

I really had a scare today. When I went to the hospital at 2:00 p.m., I found a totally drugged and asleep Dion. I tried to wake him, but I couldn't. The doctor came and asked to talk to me in private. He said Dion had taken a turn for the worse: low platelets, kidney failure, low albumin. The doctor said they were moving him back into intensive care. He indicated that Dion might not live through the shunt surgery. He added that he was almost guaranteed not to last long enough for a liver transplant.

I left the hospital feeling completely alone - as I do when I think Dion has died. But, at 5:30 p.m., Dion paged me. He said he was hungry; would I bring him some fried chicken.

I raced back to the hospital with a dinner of his favorite chicken. When the doctors came around 7:30 p.m., they were amazed at his recovery. They decided to not move him into intensive care after all.

This was the first night that I think I believed what Dion had always said to me when he said, "Since I have met you, I want to live."

I have been having some mighty powerful conversations with God; and, also I take one day at a time.

There is a mysterious and miraculous absence of Jessie.

August 15, 19_ - Saturday

Dion called me this morning to say the hospital tried to draw blood but there wasn't enough moisture in his body to make blood. He is dangerously close to being dehydrated because the albumin in his system drains into his abdominal cavity: a condition of the ascites.

He is almost too sick to live through the shunt that will stop this drainage. But, he is too sick not to get the shunt. Every ounce of liquid he drinks bypasses all of his cells and goes right to his abdomen. Meanwhile (I noticed this yesterday when helping change his pajamas) since his

134

liver cannot make protein anymore, he is all bone. He literally looks like a walking skeleton. He looks like a holocaust survivor except with a huge belly.

But, he still has those eyes and that mind I love so much. I wish he had that Scottish twinkle, but he doesn't smile much anymore. Sometimes when he looks at me, his eyes mist over and I know he loves me; and, he comes out with something like, "You still have those beautiful lips."

Jessie paged me late in the day to ask about Dion. I guess she did have a heart attack or some sort of a temporary debilitating condition that kept her away. She expressed anger at Dion for being ill and not communicating with her and asking about HER health. I wanted to say, 'well, babe, that's just how the heart valve crumbles.'

August 16, 19_ - Sunday

Tonight was difficult. I don't know if Dion felt he was going to die, but he seemed to have a lot on his mind. I asked him to please talk to me. He said he had tried telling me certain things, but I refused to listen. I said, "Please, try again."

He said that for all of my talk of love and spiritual values, I held onto things that meant nothing and put a price on priceless things. This was a comment regarding my constant preoccupation with garage sale items (which I thought had value) versus the human spirit (which he said I felt was dispensable).

He told me he had been in pain about my refusing to take his last name. He said it hurt him that I refused to let our home reflect his taste in decor. He also said that he felt I was always finding a way to get away from him.

I listened to him; and, yes, I felt guilt. But, I did not attempt to defend myself. For once, I agreed to look in the mirror. He was right about it all. It is no wonder he didn't feel loved by me no matter how many times I told him I loved him.

August 17, 19_ - Monday

I went to the hospital today, but Dion slept so soundly that I came home to run errands. He called at 5:30 p.m.; had just awakened; and talked very encouragingly. He said he thought we could be a family again. He said he couldn't wait to get home, that we would be "okay." When I remarked on his upbeat attitude as compared to last night, he said, "You allowed me to get some things off my chest; and, I feel better."

After my conversation with Dion, Jessie called. She completely ignored the news that he will be coming back home to be with me and kept talking about finding a 'place to put him.' She realizes he does not intend to stay at her house. Also, she is very disappointed to find out that much of the things that she had assumed to be factual were, in fact, not so.

Today was a delightful day spent with Dion. He, now 11 days sober, has finally become human. This is the first day he has looked well; has eaten well; and has a happy attitude. He said today is the first day he has had hope. He talked about going to AA!

He acted like the old Dion. He said, "My beauty (another name he called me) didn't like me; so, I began not to like myself."

I shutter to think how much pain he was in at my hands. I did a lot of complaining about him. I treated him as if Dion, the man, was responsible for his behavior. Really, Dion the Alcoholic was the culprit.

I didn't realize how many self-loathing and guilty feelings alcoholics feel. He didn't need me, "his beauty," adding fuel to the fire.

Jessie worries me. She is clearly very angry with Dion. She talks about him like he is already dead or is deranged. She says things like, "finding a place to put him," and "what to do with the body."

August 20, 19_ - Thursday

I worked today, but yesterday I spent all day at the hospital. When I got ready to leave, Dion got moody. I expressed dismay that I feel no matter how much I do, it isn't enough.

He said, "I just miss you when you are gone." Then he said, "please don't put me down and I won't put you down." Sounded like a reasonable request.

When I turned to leave, he held out his hand. I walked back and took his hand. He said, "I've always felt inferior to My Beauty. I never felt like she was proud of me." Then he said with every bone of kindness within him, "But, I never gave her a reason to be proud of me, did I?"

I bent down, and with tears in my eyes, I hugged his thin, thin body. We had achieved a rare breakthrough. We were finding ways to communicate at last.

He said he had decided to go through with the shunt operation, which let me know that he had decided to definitely not drink. They had told him if he had the shunt he would die instantly if he took even one drink.

He looks pretty frail. Sometimes I think the doctors know there is only a small chance he will come through the surgery, but he almost has no choice. Also, they seem to have taken a special interest in him. Either that or he is some sort of a case history.

August 21, 19_ - Friday

Dion came through the surgery fine.

August 23, 19_ - Sunday

This morning around 9:30 a.m., I got a page from Dion while I was at McDonalds with the kids. I called him back. I said, "Dion, they said a side effect of the surgery would be confusion; but, you don't sound confused to me. And, you weren't too confused to dial my number."

He said, "I'm confused enough to know that I love you." Then he did something very odd for him. He made a joke. He said, "this thing is a pain in my neck."

I said, "Oh, does your neck hurt?"

He laughed and said, "That's a joke. Don't you get it. This thing is in my neck. It's a pain in the neck."

I said, "I will be to the hospital as soon as I drop off the kids."

August 24, 19_ - Monday

After seeing Dion today, I was in total shock. He WAS confused. He didn't know where he was. He barely seemed to recognize me. He couldn't drink water without spilling it. Yes, after the shunt, his belly went down, but my Dion was gone.

Unable to reach any of his doctors or anyone, who could console me, I began to read the book of Job and to pray and sob uncontrollably. I begged God to bring Dion back. I can't imagine life without him. I confessed my greatest sin - resentment of Jessie. Suddenly, I found strength enough to quit crying. After raising holy hell on the phone, I finally got one of the doctors to call me back. Their prognosis: the hepatic encephalopathy that happens in 10 percent of shunt surgeries had happened to my Dion. They promised to put him on oxygen and promised that two doctors would check on him during the night.

Dion is in God's hands now. I have let him go and am leaning entirely on God's strength, wisdom, prompting and Divine Will.

One thing noteworthy today was that Dion knew me; and, even got himself out of bed to go to the physical therapy session he had scheduled. That was how determined he was to get his strength back. But, once in the physical therapy room, they took one look at him and knew he wasn't strong enough to work on it. He could barely walk across the room. They asked him if he wanted to do a little physical therapy or go back to the room. He said in barely audible tones, "Go back to the room."

As long as I live, I will continue to be haunted at seeing My Knight reduced to this weak, yet still-proud man, who was forced, there in the Physical Therapy Room, finally to admit defeat.

Once back in bed, he began his descent into his coma-like state.

August 25, 19_ - Tuesday

After it became obvious yesterday that Dion was failing fast, I awoke this morning from a dream where Dion had let me know that they had just left him in the room to die.

I had come home early specifically to get in touch with a doctor. When I finally managed to contact a doctor they promised me they would: 1) move him into intensive care; 2) put him on intravenous food; 3) check on him often in the night. But, in this dream, Dion's spirit was letting me know they had shoved him in a room crowded with three other men; and, left him to die.

As soon as I awoke from the dream, I called in the middle of the night and talked to the night nurse.

When asked if he had improved, she said no. When asked if doctors checked on him in the night, she said she didn't know. When asked about

137

his prognosis she huffily informed me she couldn't tell me anymore.

I threw on some clothes; raced to the hospital; ran into his room and saw my beloved husband strapped down in the bed, diaper on, oxygen in his nose. Also, he seemed out of his head. What a sad, swift change had transpired from yesterday. The nurses and doctors (because of my threats and screaming) gathered around him and made plans to usher him up to intensive care. But, I almost knew it was too late.

I think Dion recognized me because in his garbled voice I thought I could understand him to say, "Honey, help me. Help me get up."

His eyes, half closed, really opened wide; and, he looked almost frightened when I leaned over and whispered, "You are such a good soldier."

He raised up and said a loud, "No-o-o-o-o!" as if to say, 'I am no soldier. I have lost the battle. I am dying.'

It broke my heart watching him die like this: frightened, out of his head, strapped down, unable to speak clearly. Is this the best care the VA Hospital can give our veterans? Aren't these the men who risked their lives in stupid wars? Do only the wealthy earn the right to die with dignity?

I prayed all evening. I could not face that Dion was dying. Only God would be able to convince me of that.

August 26, 19_ - Wednesday

Dion died at 3:03 a.m. this morning. As with everything concerning Dion, I let him down even in his death. Having watched him come back from death for me so many other times before, and having been convinced that he would do it once again, I had left his side in the intensive care unit at 1:00 a.m. that morning, telling the nurse I was going home to get some sleep and would come back in the morning.

Even in death, I took him for granted. I assumed he would still be alive when I decided to come waltzing in, in the morning at a time convenient for me. He was dead when I arrived.

Many times Dion had said to me, "Have you noticed you are never around when important things happen to me?"

Translated, that meant the same thing then as it did now: I was never there for Dion. That I let him die alone because I needed rest will haunt me the rest of my life.

Dion may have died thirty minutes before I could get to him, but his spirit waited for me. This became obvious to me when I looked at him.

I could have sworn that he was only asleep. I touched him; he felt warm. I leaned over him, kissed him, and talked to him as if to wake him. The nurse asked me if I wanted a moment alone. I said yes. She left. But, when I turned back around, I could see that whereas Dion had been there when I first walked into the room, he was now gone. Whereas he once looked like my Dion, he now looked like a corpse. But, he HAD waited for me. I began to sob.

I hung my head and started to weep uncontrollably. I said, "I didn't think you would die. I'm not ready to lose you. You were always my brave soldier. You always pulled through for me before. I didn't think you would die and leave me like this."

August 27, 19__ - Thursday

One of my biggest mistakes in life has been not listening to my heart. I have listened to friends, family, Dr. Laura, every self-help book on the market, and any person's opinion but my own. For most of my life, I have completely ignored that still, small voice inside that we all have.

My heart knew I loved Dion, but I let the boyfriend tell me Dion was a manifestation of my own sickness (insecurity). My heart knew Dion was a good person; but, I let the pawnshop owners tell me he owed everyone in town. I let my kids tell he he was evil; I let Mother tell me, "don't get involved with a drunk." I let my friends tell me, "he looks ill." Consequently, Dion and I lost many good moments because half of me apologized for him while the other half was crazy in love with him.

My heart knew that "tough love" wouldn't work on him. He needed acceptance, not more rejection. I listened to the therapist, to the pastor when he suggested, "tell him he can come home only when he quits drinking."

When I put him out of the house this last time, my heart knew he would lose his will to live. I can only find one thing to be thankful for in all of this: Dion felt my acceptance and unconditional love near the end. As far as he knew, he would be coming back home; and we would, indeed, be a happy family. We would make it. We would live happily ever after.

Dion's death makes no sense to me. I need him. I don't want to live without him. My life makes no sense without him. I want to be with him more than I want to be with anyone who lives on the Earth today.

The only thing able to put an end to my sobbing was a call from the Bishop at the Mormon Church. Funny, I have been baptized in the church all these years, but I have been inactive. Yet, I always go back to the church in my darkest times of need because they always come through.

The Bishop said to me, "after you wait a year from Dion's death, you can go to the temple and seal your marriage for time and eternity."

This made sense to me. Many times Dion had said to me with that mysterious twinkle in his eye, "My love is eternal."

I believe Dion, a practicing Catholic, knew in his heart that our marriage was for eternity.

I said to the Bishop, "that makes more sense than anything I have heard all day because in my soul, I know that Dion was and is my eternal husband."

Dion's sandals, socks, and cigarettes lay on the bedroom floor. These are only a few things of his that I have. Naturally, Jessie has everything else. Pain stabs my heart every time I look at them; yet, I am unable to move them. I have been unable to get off the bed. I have conducted every funeral arrangement, every family notification; have done every manner of business laying here in my bed because I am unable to move.

Jessie wants back the ring she bought that he wore as our wedding ring. I offered to buy it from her. But, she won't allow me to.

I made the mistake of telling Jessie I didn't think I would ever meet anyone like Dion. She said, "Let's hope not." She just had to drop her final acid thoughts on the comment.

I will never again open myself up to her as long as I live.

August 31, 19__ - Monday

I took care of so many final details Wednesday, the day Dion died while completely in shock. Actually, having all those phone calls to make helped me grieve because to each person with whom I spoke, I told the same story over and over: "Dion didn't want to go through with the surgery. At the last minute he wanted to back out, but I talked him out of it. I thought he would recover from surgery because he had always come back from death before. I thought he was invincible. My rationale for surgery was that the shunt would buy him six more months until he could get a transplant. But, I forgot one detail more important than his strong Scottish will: his incredible survival instinct. At the last minute, his survival instinct told him not to have the surgery." And on and on I talked.

SEPTEMBER TWO

September 1, 19_ - Tuesday

Dion speaks as he sleeps. Even in death, we disagree. I want to keep his ashes in the container, add a rose and a few pictures of me that he especially loved; and set the whole works out to float in the great Atlantic Ocean. He, on the other hand, had requested his ashes be spread into the ocean by the beach where we spent two glorious weeks.

His voice is louder in death, as it should have been in life. I recognize that this obsession of mine to keep his ashes together is merely a refusal to give him up. Adding the small rose is a last attempt of mine to say, "Dion, do you remember when you gave me a rose like this? You bought it when we stopped at a gas station coming back from the beach. We had used my credit card to charge our way back home; and, I let my preoccupation with how freely you spent money overshadow how special it was to be handed a rose by you. We got into a fight; vowed we were through for 15 minutes down the road while Steve drove the van silently through our fight because he had seen so many of these fights before. He knew they were as curious as sunshine and rain.

We had also bought chicken that day at the gas station; and, I had my finger pinching off a piece of white meat when you turned around and looked at me with those forgiving Scottish eyes; and, you shook your head. A smile played at your lips as you said, "there ought to be a law ....." (against anyone being as beautiful as you are).

I took your hand then and crawled into your lap in the front seat while Steve sped down the road ignoring two fools so in love that they were kissing as if they had just met. Then we sang songs and Steve joined in. He smiled as he sang and looked straight ahead at the road as if he and the road shared secrets.

September 2, 19_ - Wednesday

I have all but quit my job. I told them I was sick; then I got in the car and set out for the beach. I drove until I got sleepy. Afraid I would go to sleep at the wheel, I checked myself into a hotel room an hour outside of town. I will get up early in the morning and continue to the beach.

September 3, 19__ - Thursday

This morning I arrived at the beach and parked the car on the spot where we camped exactly one and one-half years ago. There were a couple of people walking down a path; but, fortunately there were not many people around to watch me walk out onto the beach with your ashes in my arms.

When I walked into the water, I found it cool and not very choppy. The sun was coming up. It was a beautiful day for a burial. I opened the box with reluctance. To let the last part of you go requires tremendous faith on my part that God will gather you back to me at the last trump.

When I let trickle into the ocean your ashes, they seemed to s⌐

a fish taking to the water. You were always at home near the water, my love. I know this.

After I had let go of the last small grain of you, I watched quickly the waves welcome you home.

After the last ash, I threw into the water the rose. Then I called out to you, "Swim, my little Pisces, swim. Swim in death as you never could in life."

EPILOGUE

One year after Dion's death, I had an occasion to talk to a spiritual advisor, who told me she had a message from Dion. I include this because I feel it is only fair that you, the reader, should hear Dion's side of this, our love story.

He said, "I loved her from the moment I laid eyes on her. I loved to just look at her. She gave me the happiest moments of my life. She extended my life a year and half longer than it would have been had we not met. However, I always knew I would meet her. She was the love I always waited for."

Then, he said, "My name for her is still the name of a flower. But, my name for her is no longer Rose because a rose has thorns, and she has no thorns. My name for her is Lily. A lily is white, soft, and beautiful. It is slender and reaches up into heaven."

After the advisor opened her eyes she looked directly at me and said, "I don't think this has ever happened to me before."

The advisor could NOT have known the significance of the "flower" name had she not actually HEARD from Dion because NO ONE ever knew that he called me by the name of a flower.

I only include this epilogue to let you know that Dion lives. He loves me still from the other dimension. And, our love even continues to evolve because now he has renamed me. This doesn't surprise me because I realize that he has now begun to see with spiritual eyes; and, spiritual eyes see the most clearly of all.